Barrie Gordon PhD

Barrie is a Senior Lecturer in health and physical education at the Victoria University of Wellington, New Zealand.

He has a life time interest in fast pitch softball having played for many years, including several in the New Zealand national league. He worked as a high school physical education teacher before travelling to the USA in 1992 to complete a Masters in physical education at The Ohio State University. It was at this time that he became interested in baseball, an interest he has maintained ever since.

Barrie has a specific interest in coaching and teaching in ways that facilitate greater engagement and understanding by the players. Developing these attributes is central to the Developing Thinking Players (DTP) concept that forms the core of the DTP coaching and teaching programme.

Publishing info

All rights reserved. This book or any portion thereof may not be reproduced or used in any manner whatsoever without the express written permission of the publisher except for the use of brief quotations in a book review.

Designed by Graphic Solutions Ltd

First Printing, 2015

ISBN 978-0-473-32822-1

©Developing Thinking Players (DTP) Ltd

www.thinkingplayers.com

DEVELOPING THINKING PLAYERS

CONTENTS

PAGE 5
Introduction

PAGE 6
The underpinning principles of DTP

Principle One:

If players are to become good decision makers they need to practice making decisions in realistic contexts.

Principle Two:

For players to learn at a deeper level they must be practically involved in the coaching/learning process.

Principle Three:

The motivation to learn physical skills is enhanced when players understand why they are important within the game context.

Principle Four:

Competition is a strong motivator for players and it is important in the training phase to help replicate the competitive pressure faced in games.

Principle Five:

DTP is not a difficult approach to use and can be implemented by all coaches with success.

Principle Six:

A positive team culture is important

PAGE 11
How to implement the scenario based program

Standard method of implementing a DTP coaching session

Discussion

PAGE 15
Skill development

Variations

Develop own outcomes and points

Infield only

Rapid-fire scenarios

Maintain the same scenario

PAGE 17
Scenarios

The following pages contain 25 game play scenarios, all of these scenarios are available for download, two copies of each will be required in order for both batting and fielding teams of formulate a game plan.

PAGE 68
Overview of scenarios

PAGE 71
Developing your own scenario

At the end of this book you will find ten empty templates that you can use to develop your own scenarios. These could be developed as a result of a specific situation that occurred in a game that you would like to revisit or simply an area that you are interested in.

INTRODUCTION

All coaches and players want to be involved with teams that are successful both on and off the field. To achieve success is not always easy and requires a range of different factors to come into alignment. Some of these factors can be influenced by the coach, while others such as injuries and the calls that officials make are largely outside the coach's control. One major area where coaches can make a difference is in the way they choose to run their team practices. There is no "right way" to coach and good coaches will implement a range of approaches based on their own knowledge and background and what they perceive are the teams needs.

Team practices are important because this is the time when a team develops their understanding of tactics and teamwork and when individual players have the opportunity to remediate their weaknesses, attitudinal or skill. It is also time for the team to develop that sense of "team", an attribute that is both difficult to define but can be readily identified in successful teams.

The Developing Thinking Players (DTP) coaching program is a unique approach that will help coaches to generate success for the team and for individual players. Players participate in game scenarios that mimic real life game situations. The scenarios are played out as in a real game and the fielding and batting teams are then awarded points depending on the outcomes of the play. DTP is based on the belief that appropriate coaching can encourage every player to develop a greater understanding of the game. When players have developed this deeper understanding it brings an extra dimension to their play. We all know of players who have a real feel for the game, who understand it in ways that lead to them making good decisions and making the great plays at crucial times. But how do they develop this understanding? Are they born with a special level of interest that leads to them becoming "students of the game" or is this understanding developed through good coaching and game experience?

The DTP approach is designed to encourage players to think about their game and to make smart decisions in a range of scenarios. It is not a silver bullet that will magically transform all players into truly great ones. What DTP does offer, however, is an opportunity to help all players to reach their real potential as athletes. This is a potential not limited to a player's physical skills but includes their "feel" for the game and their subsequent ability to play better and smarter.

DTP is based on a number of well-established coaching principles supported by a robust research base. The program owes much to the Teaching Games for Understanding (TGfU) model that has become popular within coaching and the teaching of physical education in recent years.

Coaches interested in gaining greater knowledge of TGfU may like to consider "TGfU for Teachers and Coaches" which will soon be available from Amazon. A sample section is included at the back of this book.

DTP is a different way of coaching that can be used by coaches. It is NOT intended that DTP replaces other ways of coaching, but rather that it be used in conjunction with other approaches as required. This could mean that DTP forms one part of a coaching session or the full session on some occasions. As with all coaching approaches it can be implemented, modified and used in a number of ways by coaches as suits the team needs and responses.

THE UNDERPINNING PRINCIPLES OF DTP

The DTP approach is based on six major principles. These are addressed separately below but it is important to emphasize that in reality they are combined in a variety of ways when the DTP approach is used in coaching.

Principle One:

If players are to become good decision makers they need to practice making decisions in realistic contexts.

While this may sound obvious, players are seldom placed in realistic scenarios that are designed to give them practice at reading situations, making appropriate decisions and then considering the subsequent results of their actions. When this does happen it prepares them to make better decisions in later game situations. In order to develop their ability to make good decisions it is important that players, having made the play, are given the opportunity to analyze their decision-making in relation to the consequences that result. It is the process of observing and thinking about what has occurred that generates true learning for the players.

An example of the complexity that faces players is the situation where the fielding team has a runner on three and must decide how to react. Their decision-making should be influenced by a number of external factors that need to be taken into account, often in a split second:

How many outs	How fast is the runner/ground conditions?
The score	Where is the ball hit?
The innings	Was it fielded cleanly?
Who are the next batters?	

In a tied game at the bottom of the final innings the only option is to try to stop the runner scoring.

What, however, is the smart play if the fielding team was up by three in this situation with one out and the ninth batter on deck?

What if it is the identical situation but it is the top of the final innings? Does this situation require different decision-making? What is the best outcome? The second best?

In the same situations what is the batting team hoping to achieve? Where is the best place to hit the ball? How does this change with different game contexts?

The number of different combinations that a team can potentially face is astronomical and it is therefore vital that players learn to analyze situations as they arise and develop the ability to make good decisions based on the situations they face. The DTP approach gives players this opportunity while allowing them to play out their decisions in real game scenarios. They get to decide what they want and then try to achieve the outcome in real life situations. After the action has finished they get a chance to think about what happened, what was effective and what was not. It is this process that generates a feel for the game and deeper learning.

Principle Two:

For players to learn at a deeper level they must be practically involved in the coaching/learning process.

The second principle is closely related to the first. The depth of understanding that a player develops will be influenced by the degree to which they are engaged with the learning process. In simple terms, if the coach tells players what to do they will learn at a surface level to react in certain ways. This may not serve them well when the pressure goes on in a game, or a new situation arises that they have not been prepared for. If, however, the players are encouraged to engage in thinking and contemplating, they will learn at a deeper level. This deeper learning will lead to players being better able to think through problems, have a greater understanding of the game, and be better equipped to handle real game situations in the future.

An example would be the situation of Scenario Twelve below.

	SCORE			
OUTS	FIELDING **2**	INNINGS	RUNNERS	SCENARIO
NONE	BATTING **3**	**TOP OF THREE/TWO**	**THIRD**	**12**

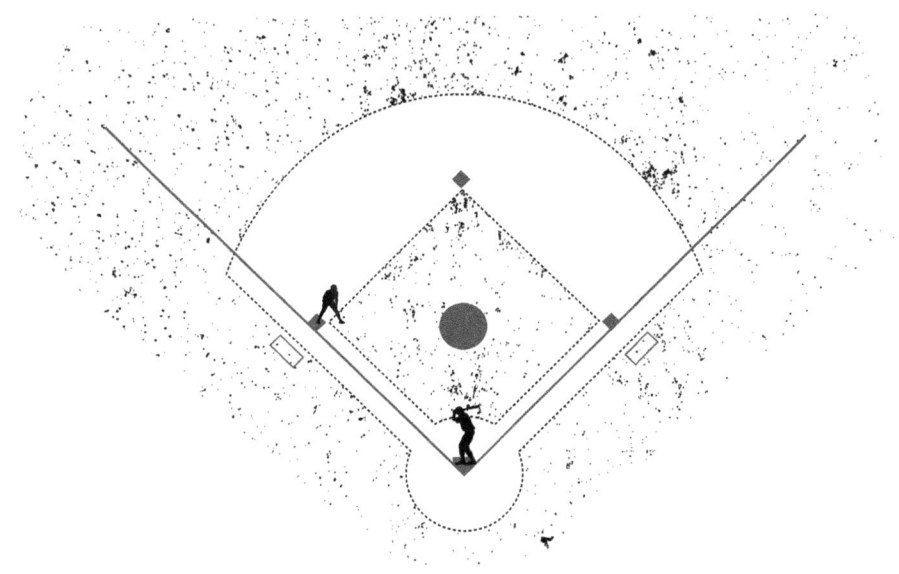

As a coach you could address this at three levels

Level one: simply tell the players what to do and get them to practice it

Level two: supply the outcomes card as below and get the players to discuss and decide how they want to play the scenario. Then allow them to try out the scenario in practice to see what happens.

Outcomes for batting and fielding teams and resultant points

Batting Team		Fielding Team	
Score run (no outs)	Three points	No run scored (one out)	Three points
Score run (one out)	Two points	No run scored runners safe Third and First	Two points
Two runners on base (no outs)	One point	No run scored runners safe Third and Second	One point

You can see that level two requires a deeper level of engagement by the players than level one.

Note: The number of outs stated in the table relates to the situation at the conclusion of the scenario. They are NOT the number of outs taken during the scenario play. There is no provision in the points table for walks. In all situations a home run is the best outcome for the batting team. In the DTP programme this is not included in the scoring tables. Having it as the number one outcome on every table would encourage batters to try to hit the ball out of the park every time they batted. The DTP programme encourages batters to be strategic in where and how they hit rather than going for the fence on every occasion. If a batter does hit a home run during play then they should be awarded the maximum three points. If it occurs when playing an infield only game, a ball hit into the outfield on the full is batter out. A ball hit through the infield is a two hit base hit. In level three, the option below where players develop their own criteria, explain that a home run should not be the three point score for the batting team.

Level three: Give players scenario twelve, as above, but give them a blank outcomes for batting and fielding teams sheet as below:

Batting Team		Fielding Team	
	Three points		Three points
	Two points		Two points
	One point		One point

Then ask the players to discuss and come up with their own outcomes for three, two and one points. This forces a greater engagement with the scenario and a deeper understanding of the different possibilities in any situation. Again, allow them to try out the scenario in practice to see what happens.

This knowledge base will be useful when they face this or similar situations in real games.

Note blank outcome tables for all scenarios can be downloaded from the DTP website www.thinkingplayers.com

There are many opportunities for a coach who values and understands the need to engage players cognitively to do so when using the DTP program. Other examples of these opportunities will be clearly identified throughout the book. Unexpected opportunities will also emerge as the DTP program is implemented and coaches should take advantage of these as they occur.

Principle Three:

The motivation to learn physical skills is enhanced when players understand why they are important within the game context.

Coaches have traditionally taught skills in isolation first and then supplied opportunities for players to practice these skills in small or full game contexts. The DTP approach asks a fundamental question: "why do we coach *how* before the players know *why*"? The lack of a compelling answer to this question has led to the traditional coaching sequence being reversed in DTP. The scenario-based activities place the players in situations whereby they gain a sense of the game's tactics and gain experience in making tactical decisions. It is during this process that they learn what skills are needed to implement these decisions in practice. They also learn whether they have the particular skills necessary to successfully implement their decisions. If they lack the necessary skills then their failure to be successful in a 'real sense' is a powerful motivator to learn and practice these skills. When players can clearly see the reasons for a particular skill (and that not having it has real consequences) they become highly motivated to improve.

Example: a player in the shortstop position in scenario sixteen knows that taking a clean out at two, with an accurate, correctly paced throw, will allow for a double play and score his fielding team the maximum three points. If he throws poorly and the double is lost then he clearly knows that to achieve the double in future he will have to develop a skill set that allows him to field cleanly and throw accurately at a suitable speed. As a coach you may identify that the problem is the player's body position during the fielding phase. You now have a specific context to frame your feedback and teaching of this skill along with a player who is highly motivated to learn.

Principle Four:

Competition is a strong motivator for players and it is important in the training phase to help replicate the competitive pressure faced in games.

For this reason, the scenario-based training at the centre of DTP involves competition. It is important to acknowledge, however, that there are times when competition can have a negative effect. Teaching specific skills, for example, should be done without the distraction of competitive elements. As the skills become embedded then they can be tested and strengthened in competitive situations.

Principle Five:

The role of the coach is of paramount importance

It is important to emphasize that the DTP approach is not about reducing the role of the coach but changing it to a more effective one. For many coaches it can be difficult to accept that there are times when they should step back and let the players work things out for themselves. This is especially so when the players make decisions on tactics that the coach believes are wrong. There can be a resulting temptation to simply tell players that this is the "right way" and to get on with it. For some coaches, ego can also be involved in a way that makes it difficult for them to step back from being seen as the font of all knowledge. This stepping back process should be seen, however, as a positive action that supplies opportunities for the coach to facilitate valuable discussions about what worked well and what could be done differently.

One of the problems that coaches face when considering implementing something new is that the unfamiliar can look difficult and perhaps a little scary. This can make it tempting to stay with the tried and true, with what works and gives a degree of certainty. Unfortunately, by failing to move forward coaches can miss opportunities and end up being left behind. A coach who ignored the value of video analysis when it first became available, for example, would soon have found themselves and their team placed at a strong disadvantage. The DTP approach has elements that may differ from what many coaches are familiar with. As a result, the program may look to be difficult to implement. DTP is not a difficult approach and coaches have generally found that they can work with it easily. We would therefore encourage coaches to read the background material carefully and to then implement the process a step at a time.

Principle Six:

A positive team culture is important

For the DTP approach to be successful the team culture must support players' attempts to try new things. There must be an understanding by all involved that mistakes are OK and are the basis on which learning occurs. As a coach you do not want your players to be reluctant to push their boundaries, either because they are afraid of putdowns from teammates or of how you will respond.

Teaching players to deal with competition in a mature way is also an important role for the coach in developing and maintaining a positive team culture. Players will need to be guided firmly to ensure that they don't become driven by the competitive elements of DTP to a degree that leads to negativity. If this occurs a team culture will quickly develop that is counterproductive to players experimenting and learning successfully. Of equal importance, an overly negative climate will lead to players not enjoying their sport, which is the last thing any coach or parent wants.

HOW TO IMPLEMENT THE DTP BASED PROGRAM

There are a number of variations in the way that the scenarios provided may be used. The choice you make will depend on the number of players at practice, the level of their knowledge and your comfort with letting the players come to their own understandings. It will also be influenced by how the players respond to this approach. You may find that they are more able and willing than you expect and you may then decide to give them more input. Alternatively, you may find they are used to being told what to do and are not ready to show the level of responsibility you expect. If this occurs, you may decide to reduce their input until they have had more practice at thinking and working together and are better able to handle the approach.

How to use the DTP scenarios in a coaching session
Coaching context

You have a full squad at training and they are divided into two roughly even teams. After a warm-up and appropriate activities you should move into the DTP phase. You explain that this is a competition between the two teams and the winner is the first to reach twenty-one points (or a number selected for the time available)

The fielding team decides on their positions and the batting team organizes its batting order as in a normal game. The first scenario is selected either by you as the coach or randomly by one of the captains. Note that for all scenarios the innings has two options e.g. Top of Nine/Seven. The first is for baseball and the second for softball. Select whichever is appropriate.

For the purposes of this example we will use scenario Six.

OUTS	SCORE FIELDING 2	INNINGS	RUNNERS	SCENARIO
TWO	BATTING 2	TOP OF FOUR/THREE	SECOND & THIRD	6

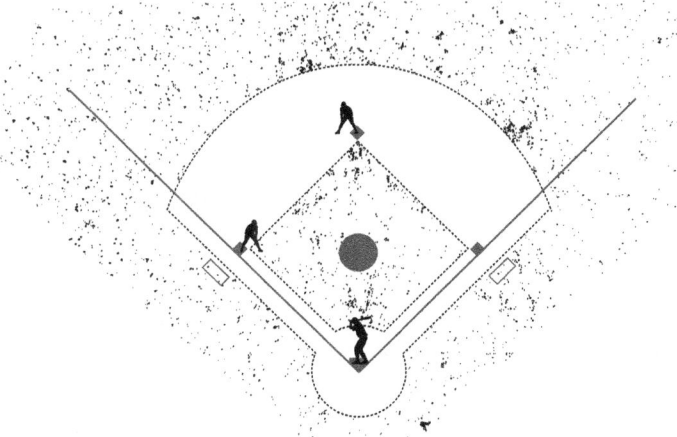

Each team is given a copy of the scenario card which explains the scenario and what outcomes both teams have to achieve in order to earn points.

Outcomes for batting and fielding teams and resultant points

Batting Team		Fielding Team	
Score two runs	Three points	No run scored (three out)	Three points
Score one run	Two points	No run scored – loaded bases	Two points
Loaded bases (two out)	One point	Run scored then third out taken	One point

Once the teams have read the scenario card, give them time to discuss what the best way is to maximize their chance to score maximum points and to minimize the opposition's scoring.

Questions to help generate discussion

Fielding team	Batting team
What is the situation?	What is the situation?
What do we want to achieve?	What do we want to achieve?
How best can we achieve this?	Where is the best place to hit the ball?
What will we do if the ball is hit to ....?	What do the runners need to do to achieve the best result?
What will I do if the ball is hit to ....?	
If we can't achieve three points what is our back-up plan to ensure two or at least one point?	What is our second plan if the first doesn't work?
What decisions do I need to make as an individual player?	

If you disagree with what they have decided at this point don't tell them but let them play through the scenarios. You will have an opportunity to discuss the decisions that the players have made at the completion of the game.

The intent is for the scenarios to generate opportunities for decision making and practical involvement. For that reason it is important that each batter hits the ball and brings about a response from the fielding team. You therefore need to structure the scenarios in a way that ensures this happens. Three suggestions are:

1: Bat off a batting tee, which gives the batting team full control of where they are going to hit it.

2: Have a pitcher who is of reasonable ability but not overpowering for the batters. You want a pitcher who can pitch strikes regularly and give lots of opportunities for batters to hit.

3: Have a member of the batting team pitch to his or her own team. Have a fielder stand next to them to play the fielding role.

The batting team supplies runners as the scenario designates and it's:

The scenario is then played out with the coach keeping score. Once the play is finished both the batting and fielding teams discuss what happened and whether they need to make changes.

During this phase it's again important that as the coach you don't dominate the discussion. Allow the discussion to run its course and if the players decide on different tactics to what you think is best, avoid the temptation to overrule them. All decisions and the reasons for them can be revisited in the discussion phase at the completion of the game.

The scenario is then reset and repeated twice more. The next batters in the roster come up to bat and the last batters become runners each time.

After three plays the batting and fielding team swap, a new scenario is selected, and the process is repeated. Alternate the batting and fielding teams in this way, with a different scenario each time, until one team gets to twenty-one points and becomes the winner.

Discussion

At the completion of the game, call the teams in and ask them if they have specific scenarios they would like to discuss. This is a **crucial** phase because you want your players to reflect on the various scenarios so that they develop a deeper understanding of the game.

Each scenario has a page attached for the coach to use to help guide the discussion, to make notes for later, and to identify specific skills that need development.

One basic sequence that you can work with is the following:

- In that last play what did you do well?
- If you had to repeat the play what (if anything) would you do differently?
- This could look something like:
  - In the scenario where there was a runner on Third and none down what did you do well (fielding team - batting team)?
  - Having thought about it, what would you do differently next time? Why?

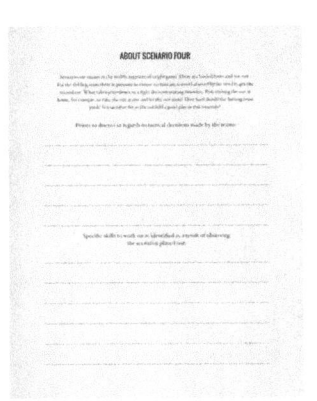

Coaching sheet example

You can then lead a discussion about particular scenarios that they/you want to revisit. There can be a temptation to concentrate on situations where things went wrong in order to fix them. These certainly need to be addressed but there should be a balance between "problems" and discussing what went well. This serves the purpose of reinforcing good play and generating a positive belief in the players. Sometimes when things go well players are not sure why and so a positive discussion can lead to the success being repeated.

- In the last play... That is exactly what we wanted to happen. What did you do to get this result? How could we increase the chances of it happening again?
- What was so good about that last play?

It is also important that individual players think about their role. You could ask them the following and get them to explain to a team mate in pairs or small groups. This has the advantage of ensuring all players are thinking and discussing their decision making and tactical thinking whereas if they are telling the whole group one at a time, this will take longer and some players may **avoid** doing so.

- What did you do when...?
- What was your thinking when you...?
- Explain why you... What would you do next time?
- What should the player closest to the ball do if..... why?
- As a team what happens when......?

You can see that the list of questions contains a mixture of questions around good plays and plays where poor decisions or execution occurred. It is important that both aspects are covered.

When considering what has happened in the scenarios the questions can be very specific:

- In the scenario with a runner on Second and one out, you ended up with two outs and the runner still on Second. What made that happen and what did each of you do to ensure that it did? It's important we understand what went right because we want to make sure the same thing happens next time we are in that situation.
- Batting team. Where did you hit during that play? Would you hit in the same place again? Why/why not? What other options are there?

Other questions could be based on the examples given but as a coach it is important that as your experience grows you develop your own.

Let the discussion continue and add comments where appropriate to facilitate understanding, for example:

- Would this be different if it was bottom of the final innings rather than the top of third?
- What are the risks of trying to get the out at home as in the first option?
- What are the rewards?
- Would it be different if the batter on deck was their number three batter rather than their number nine? How would you react differently and why?

This is your opportunity as the coach to designate the complexity of the scenario and the resultant tactical responses. The intention of this approach is to get the players to think at a deeper level about the variety of factors that influence decision-making in any specific situation.

If there was a specific situation where you felt a different tactic was appropriate this is the time to put it out there and see what they think. Be prepared to explain why you think they should have played it differently. It is through developing an understanding of why certain approaches are more effective than others that true learning develops.

SKILL DEVELOPMENT

As explained in principle three, one of the strengths of the DTP approach is that involvement in the scenarios leads to players becoming aware of physical skills they need to improve on and increases their motivation to learn. This provides you with a golden opportunity to teach them what they need. It is important that these opportunities are taken when the players are most motivated which will be close to the time when the need is exposed. After the game, spend some time on skill development with specific emphasis on the skills identified. This can be a whole team exercise if the need has been identified, or a small group or individual practice.

Lets have a look at your throw to Second and see if we can sort out why we were missing that double play. We can spend five minutes on it now and you can practice at home. We can check your progress next practice and see how you are improving.

Variations in ways to implement DTP in your practices

There are a number of variations in the ways that you can implement the DTP approach. Four are described below but there will be others that you will develop as you become more familiar with the process. Try them and see how they work. If you develop an alternative variation that works really well let us know and we will share it with others.

Develop own outcomes and points

The first decision you need to make is whether to use the pre-developed outcomes and points or get the teams to generate their own. The advantage of getting the players to develop their own is that it will generate thinking and discussion that will lead to a greater understanding. The disadvantage is that it can take time and if not carefully monitored you can find that only a small number of players are involved in deciding, while the others are left waiting around.

An alternative is to give out a scenario at the end of practice and get the players to decide on three, two and one point outcomes for both teams before the next practice. They can bring their ideas back and you can use the various suggestions as the starting point for the discussion from there. The same process can also be used as an interesting wet-day activity.

Infield only

If player numbers are low, and you cannot field two full teams, then play two teams with infield only. The same rules are played with the exception that if the batter hits directly into the outfield they are out. If a ball is hit through the infield it is an automatic two base hit (this works well with a batting tee).

Rapid-fire scenarios

Once the players understand the scenario-based concept, you can play with a new scenario after each play. These can be random or deliberately selected by you as a coach to meet your coaching needs. After three plays have been completed then the batting and fielding teams swap and another three scenarios are played through. This introduces more variety and demands more of the players as they have to think through a variety of different scenarios. Again it is important to allow time for the teams to discuss each scenario and to identify what they consider are the best tactics in each case.

Maintain the same scenario

After the three plays are completed swap teams but maintain the same scenario. After both teams have had an opportunity to play through the scenario three times, introduce a new one.

Developing your own scenario

At the end of this book you will find ten empty templates that you can use to develop your own scenarios. These could be developed as a result of a specific situation that occurred in a game that you would like to revisit or simply an area that you are interested in. The process of developing three, two and one point outcomes could involve the players or be created by you.

An alternative use of the templates could be to give them to the players to develop for a subsequent practice. Again this cognitive engagement will help generate the deeper levels of learning that are so important to understanding the game.

SCENARIOS

The following pages contain game based scenarios. Each scenario has a points table and an attached coaching/teaching page that explains the scenario and has space for notes to be taken for future discussion.

Each scenario can also be uploaded to iPads or smart phones via the QR code.

WWW.THINKINGPLAYERS.COM/SCENARIOS

SCORE

SCENARIO	OUTS	FIELDING **4**	INNINGS	RUNNERS
1	**ONE**	BATTING **3**	**TOP OF SIX/FIVE**	**SECOND**

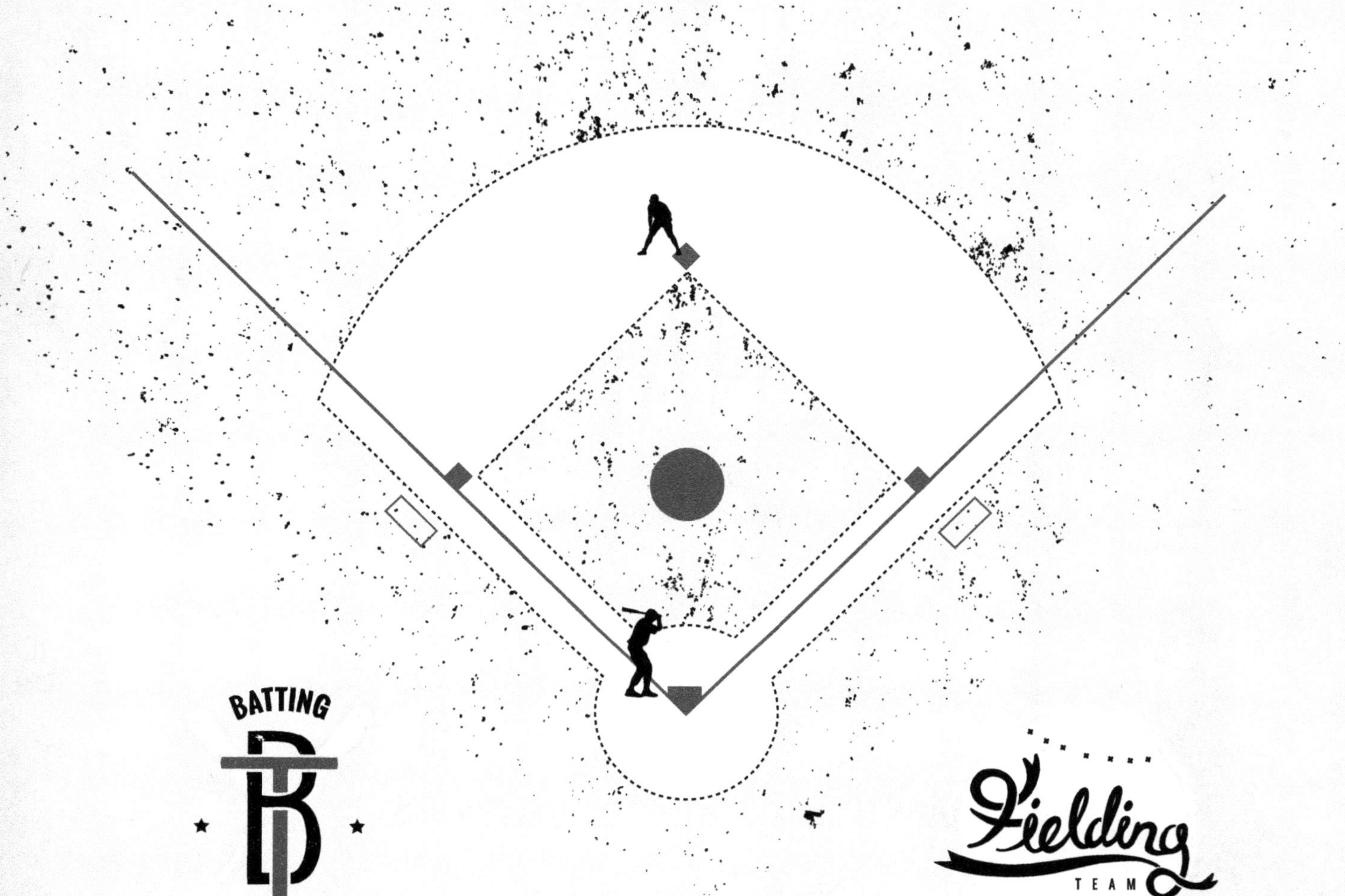

BATTING TEAM

One run scored (one out)	**3** PTS
Runner to Third (one out)	**2** PTS
Runner to Third (two outs)	**1** PT

Fielding TEAM

3 PTS	Runner on Second (two outs)
2 PTS	Runners on First and Third (one out)
1 PT	Runner on Third (two outs)

DOWNLOAD

www.thinkingplayers.com/scenarios/dtp_scenarios_1.pdf

ABOUT SCENARIO ONE

Scenario one occurs in the middle segment of a tight game. There is a runner in scoring position on Third and a chance for the batting team to tie the game. With one out the batting team must balance the advancing of the runner with the risk of a second out. The same tension occurs for the fielding team. Is it better to hold the runner at Second without getting an out or get the second out and have a runner on Third? What importance should be placed on having a potential force play at First, Second and Third if the play ends with runners on First and Second with one out?

Points to discuss in regards to tactical decisions made by the teams:

_____
_____
_____
_____
_____

Specific skills to work on as identified from observing the scenarios:

_____
_____
_____
_____
_____
_____

SCORE

SCENARIO	OUTS	FIELDING 3	INNINGS	RUNNERS
2	TWO	BATTING 3	BOTTOM OF FIVE/FOUR	FIRST

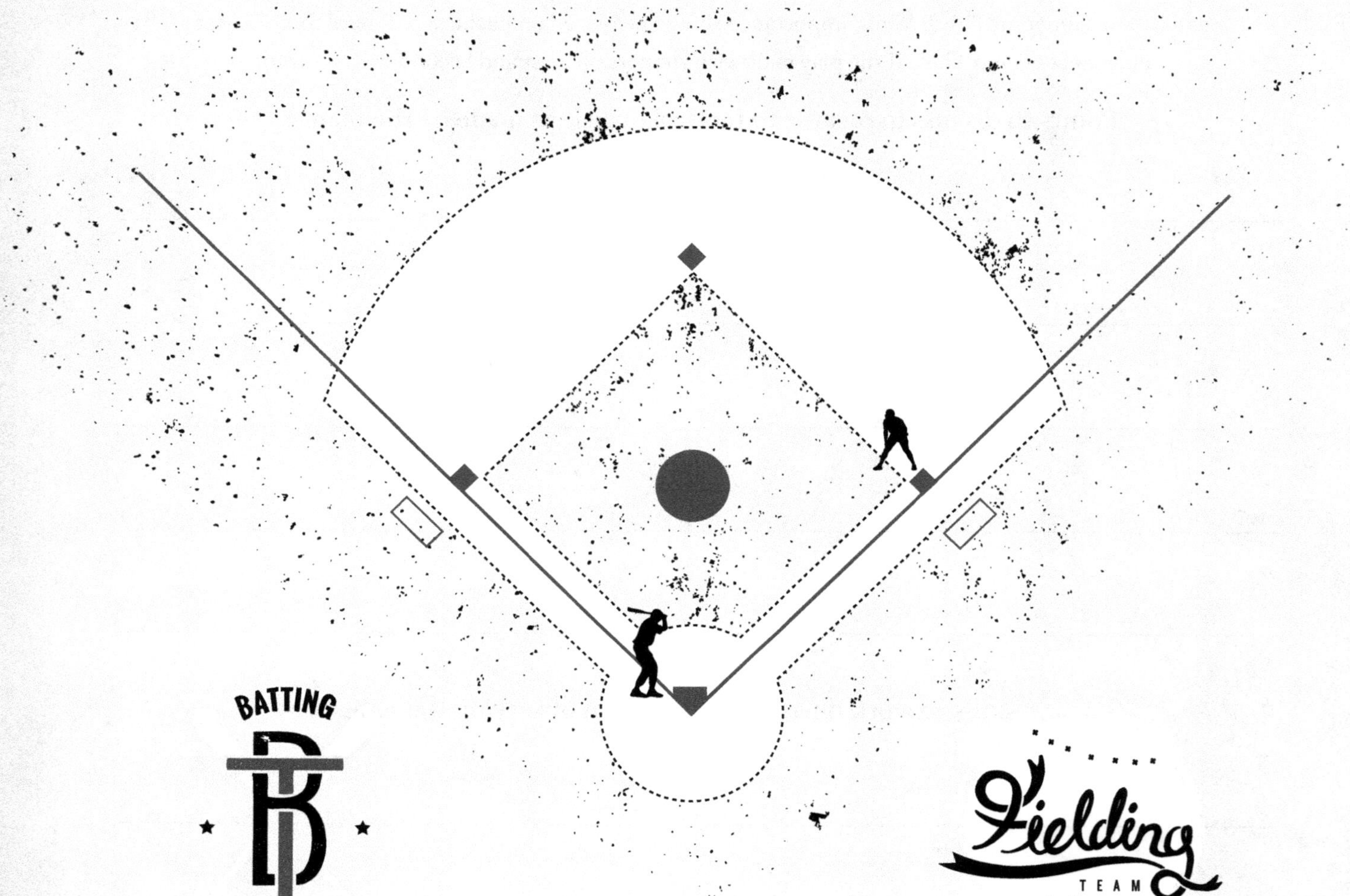

BATTING TEAM

One run scored	3 PTS
Runners safe First and Third	2 PTS
Runners safe First and Second	1 PT

Fielding Team

3 PTS	Three outs
2 PTS	Runners safe First and Second
1 PT	Runners safe First and Third

DOWNLOAD

www.thinkingplayers.com/scenarios/dtp_scenarios_2.pdf

ABOUT SCENARIO TWO

Scenario two occurs in the middle segment of a tied game. With two outs and a runner on First the advantage is with the fielding team who have only to get the third out. With a force play at Second where should the batting team be hitting? How aggressive should the runner(s) be in this situation?

Points to discuss in regards to tactical decisions made by the teams:
_____
_____
_____
_____
_____

Specific skills to work on as identified from observing the scenarios:
_____
_____
_____
_____
_____
_____

SCORE

SCENARIO	OUTS	FIELDING 5	INNINGS	RUNNERS
3	TWO	BATTING 4	BOTTOM OF NINE/SEVEN	FIRST

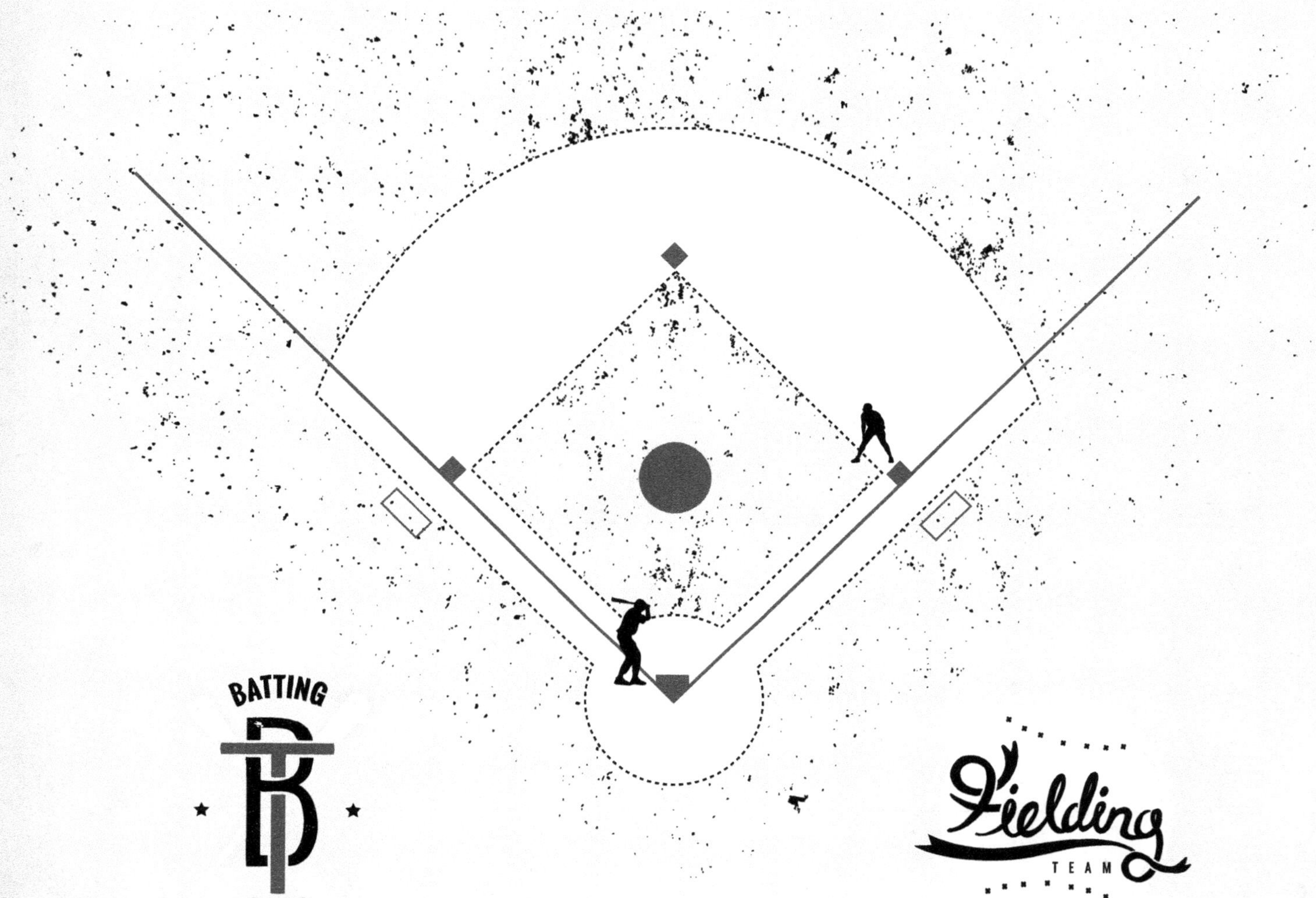

BATTING TEAM

Fielding TEAM

One run scored	**3** PTS	
Runners safe Second and Third	**2** PTS	
Runners safe First and Third	**1** PT	

DOWNLOAD

3 PTS	Three outs	
2 PTS	Runners safe First and Second	
1 PT	Runners safe Third and (First or Second)	

www.thinkingplayers.com/scenarios/dtp_scenarios_3.pdf

ABOUT SCENARIO THREE

Scenario three occurs at the bottom of the last innings. The advantage is with the fielding team but there is also substantial pressure to get the final out and to prevent the game being tied. For the batting team this is the last chance, one more out and the game is over. Where should they be hitting and how aggressive should the base runner(s) be. Is there room here for the unexpected? What is the risk and what is the reward?

Points to discuss in regards to tactical decisions made by the teams:

_____
_____
_____
_____
_____

Specific skills to work on as identified from observing the scenarios:

_____
_____
_____
_____
_____
_____

SCENARIO	OUTS	FIELDING 4	INNINGS	RUNNERS
4	ONE	BATTING 5	TOP OF FIVE/FOUR	LOADED BASES

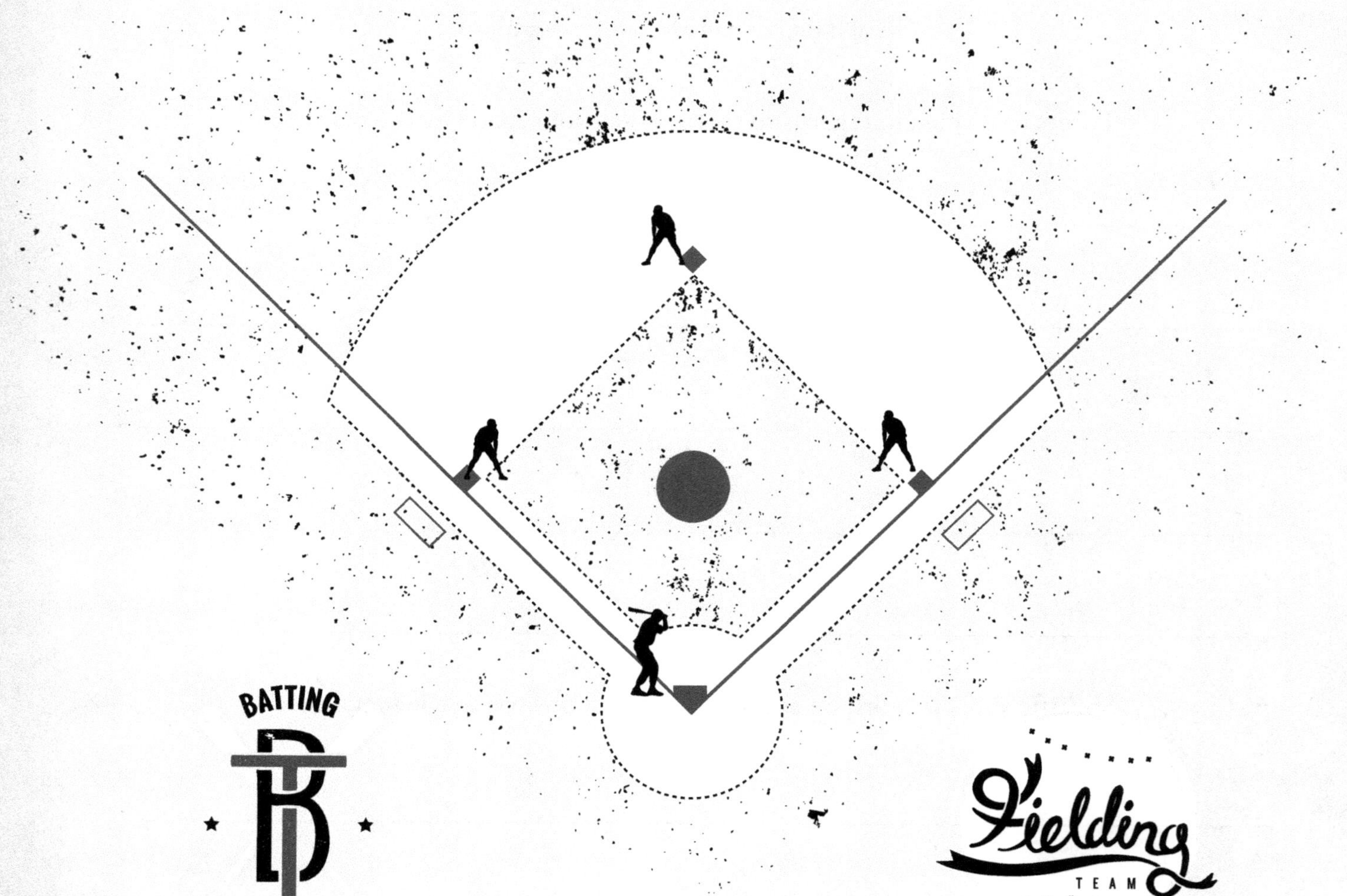

SCORE

Batting Team

Two or more runs scored (one out)	**3** PTS
One run scored (one out)	**2** PTS
One run scored (two outs)	**1** PT

Fielding Team

3 PTS	No run scored (three outs)
2 PTS	No run scored (two outs)
1 PT	One run scored (two outs)

DOWNLOAD

www.thinkingplayers.com/scenarios/dtp_scenarios_4.pdf

ABOUT SCENARIO FOUR

Scenario four occurs in the middle segment of a tight game. There are loaded bases and one out. For the fielding team there is pressure to ensure no runs are scored balanced by the need to get the second out. What takes precedence in a tight decision making situation. Risk missing the out at home, for example, or take the out at First and let the run score? How hard should the batting team push? Is a sacrifice hit to the outfield a good play in this situation?

Points to discuss in regards to tactical decisions made by the teams:

_____

_____

_____

_____

Specific skills to work on as identified from observing the scenarios:

_____

_____

_____

_____

_____

SCORE

SCENARIO	OUTS	FIELDING 10	INNINGS	RUNNERS
5	**ONE**	**BATTING 3**	**BOTTOM OF EIGHT/SIX**	**FIRST & THIRD**

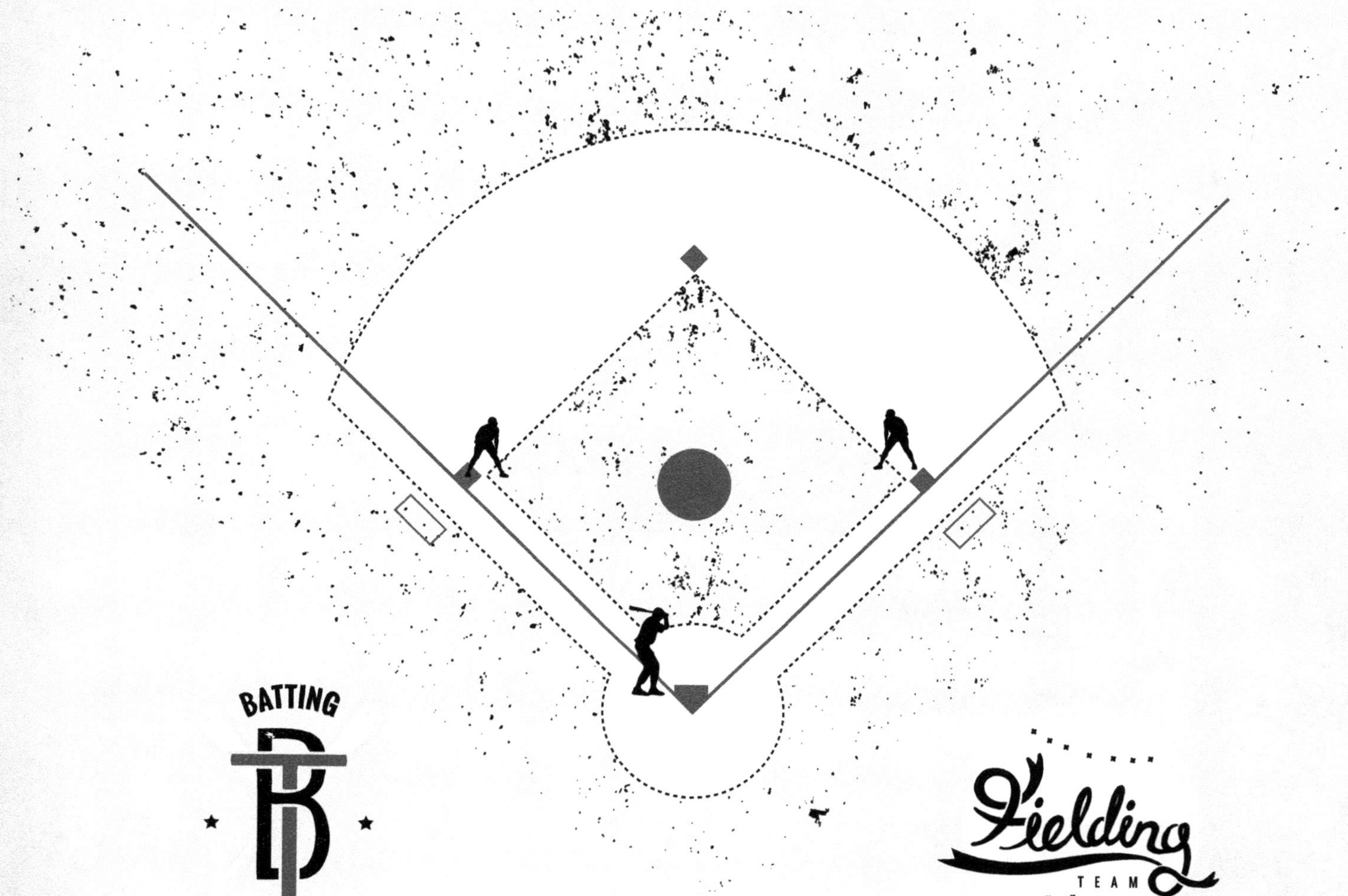

BATTING TEAM

Fielding TEAM

One run scored (one out)	**3** PTS
One run scored (two outs)	**2** PTS
Loaded bases (one out)	**1** PT

3 PTS	No run scored (three outs)
2 PTS	No run scored (two outs)
1 PT	Loaded bases (one out)

DOWNLOAD

www.thinkingplayers.com/scenarios/dtp_scenarios_5.pdf

ABOUT SCENARIO FIVE

Scenario five occurs towards the end of the game. The fielding team is up by seven runs and needs five outs for the game. Does this situation change the emphasis from preventing runs towards securing outs? In tight decision making situations does securing the out become the priority or should every attempt be made to stop the run. If the batting team were on a roll and had scored all their runs this turn at bat does this alter the thinking?

Points to discuss in regards to tactical decisions made by the teams:

_____
_____
_____
_____

Specific skills to work on as identified from observing the scenarios:

_____
_____
_____
_____
_____
_____

SCORE

SCENARIO	OUTS	FIELDING 2	INNINGS	RUNNERS
6	**TWO**	**BATTING 2**	**TOP OF FOUR/THREE**	**SECOND & THIRD**

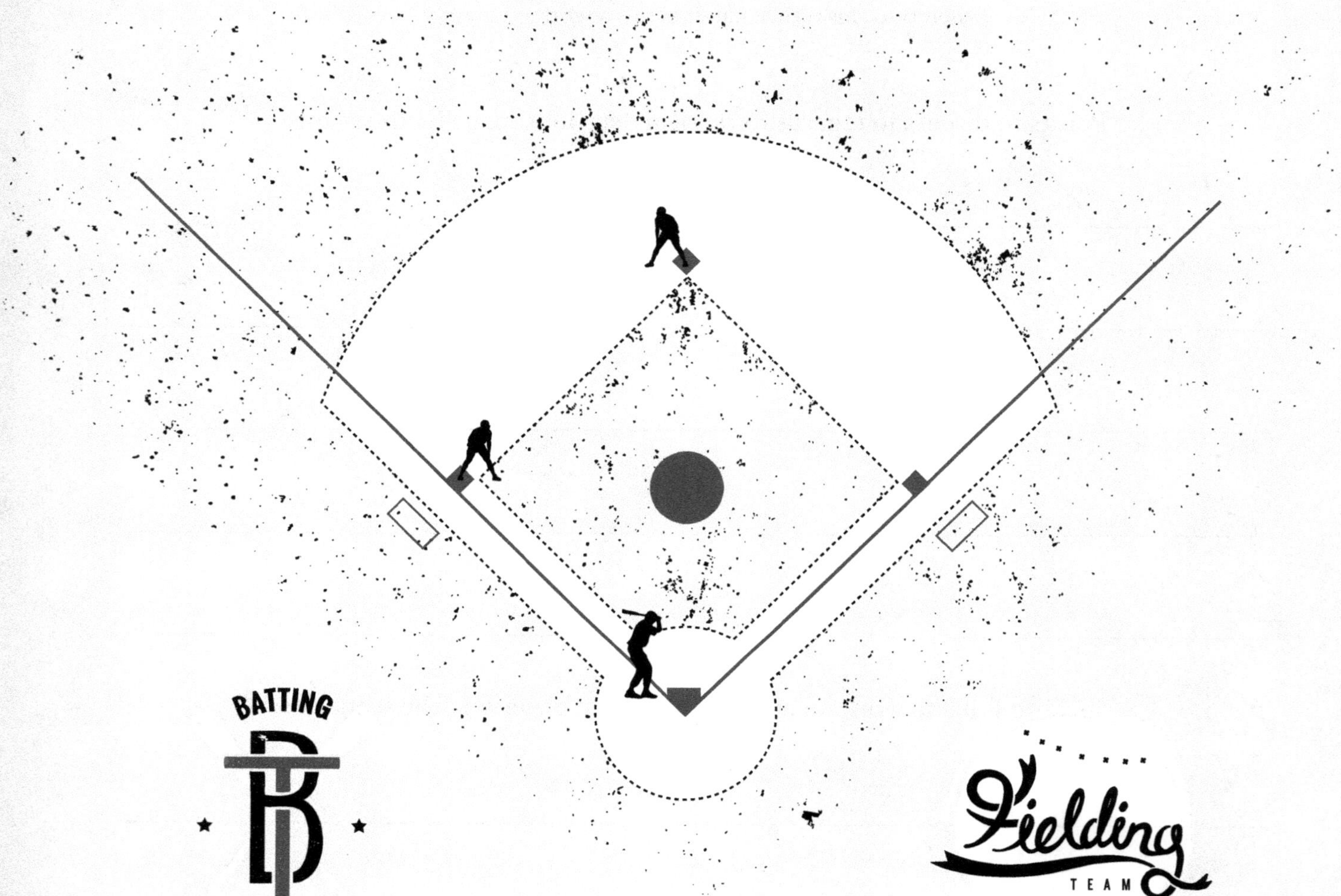

BATTING TEAM

Two runs scored	**3** PTS
One run scored	**2** PTS
Loaded bases (two outs)	**1** PT

Fielding TEAM

3 PTS	No run scored (three out)
2 PTS	No run scored loaded bases
1 PT	One run scored then third out taken

DOWNLOAD

www.thinkingplayers.com/scenarios/dtp_scenarios_6.pdf

ABOUT SCENARIO SIX

Scenario six occurs in the middle segment of a tight game. With runners on Second and Third there is only a forced play at First. Where is the best place to hit to? What is the priority for the fielding team? Is it better for them to try for the out in a tight situation or hold the throw and load the bases? How aggressive should the base runners be? In a tight situation should they take risks and put pressure on the fielding team or be careful to avoid the third out.

Points to discuss in regards to tactical decisions made by the teams:

_____
_____
_____
_____

Specific skills to work on as identified from observing the scenarios:

_____
_____
_____
_____
_____
_____

SCORE

SCENARIO	OUTS	FIELDING 7	INNINGS	RUNNERS
7	NONE	BATTING 1	BOTTOM OF EIGHT/SIX	LOADED BASES

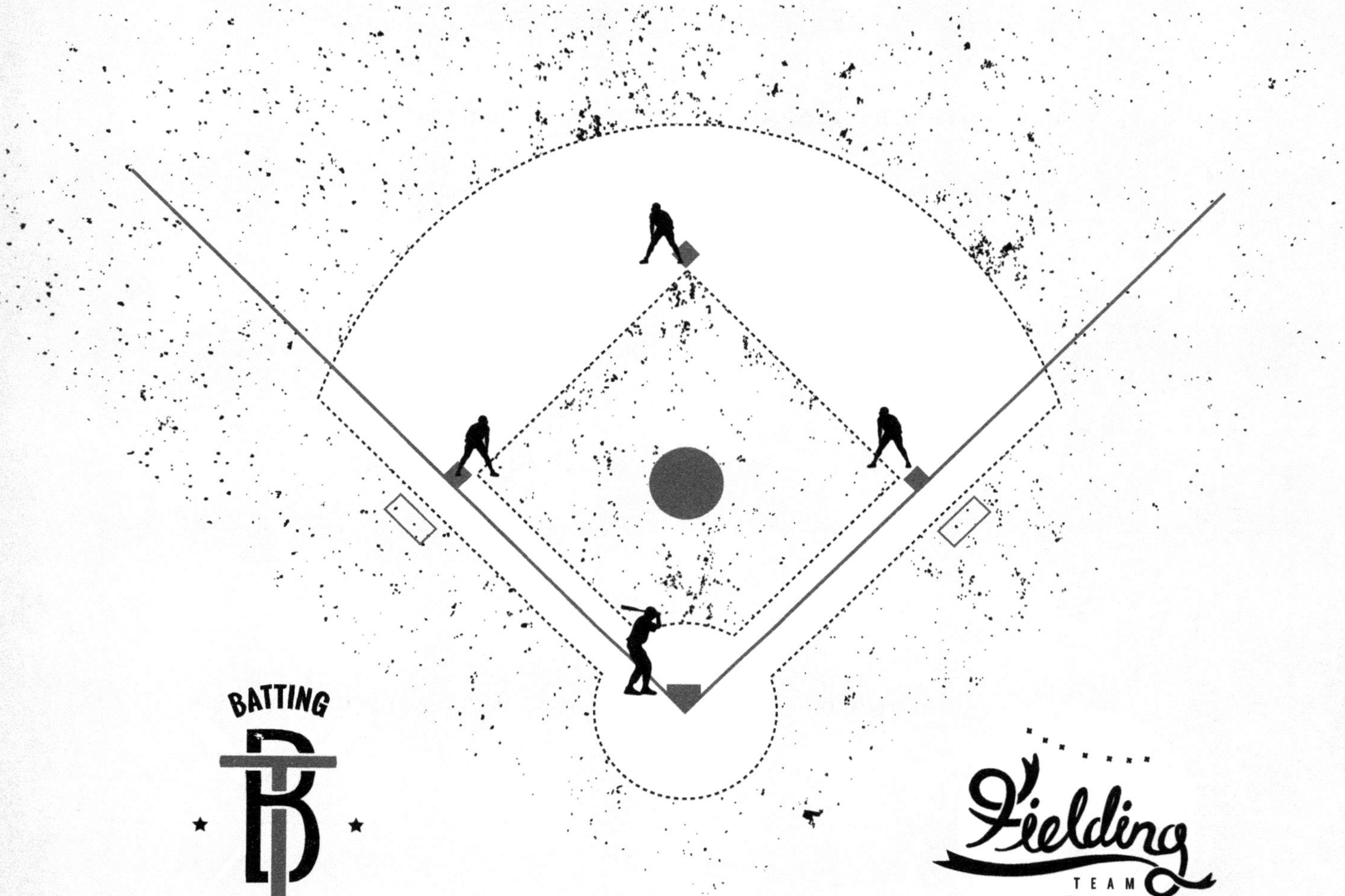

BATTING TEAM

Two or more runs scored (no outs)	**3** PTS
Two or more runs scored (one out)	**2** PTS
One run scored (no outs)	**1** PT

FIELDING TEAM

3 PTS	No run scored (two outs)
2 PTS	No run scored (one out)
1 PT	One run scored (two outs)

DOWNLOAD

www.thinkingplayers.com/scenarios/dtp_scenarios_7.pdf

ABOUT SCENARIO SEVEN

Scenario seven occurs towards the end of the game with the fielding team well ahead but facing loaded bases and no outs. What is the number one priority for the fielding team – getting outs or preventing runs. Should they take an out and let a single run score – how about if they can get two outs and give up a run(s)? What can the batting team do to try and minimize hitting into a double play?

Points to discuss in regards to tactical decisions made by the teams:
_____
_____
_____
_____

Specific skills to work on as identified from observing the scenarios:
_____
_____
_____
_____

SCORE

SCENARIO	OUTS	FIELDING 2	INNINGS	RUNNERS
8	NONE	BATTING 3	BOTTOM OF THREE/TWO	FIRST & THIRD

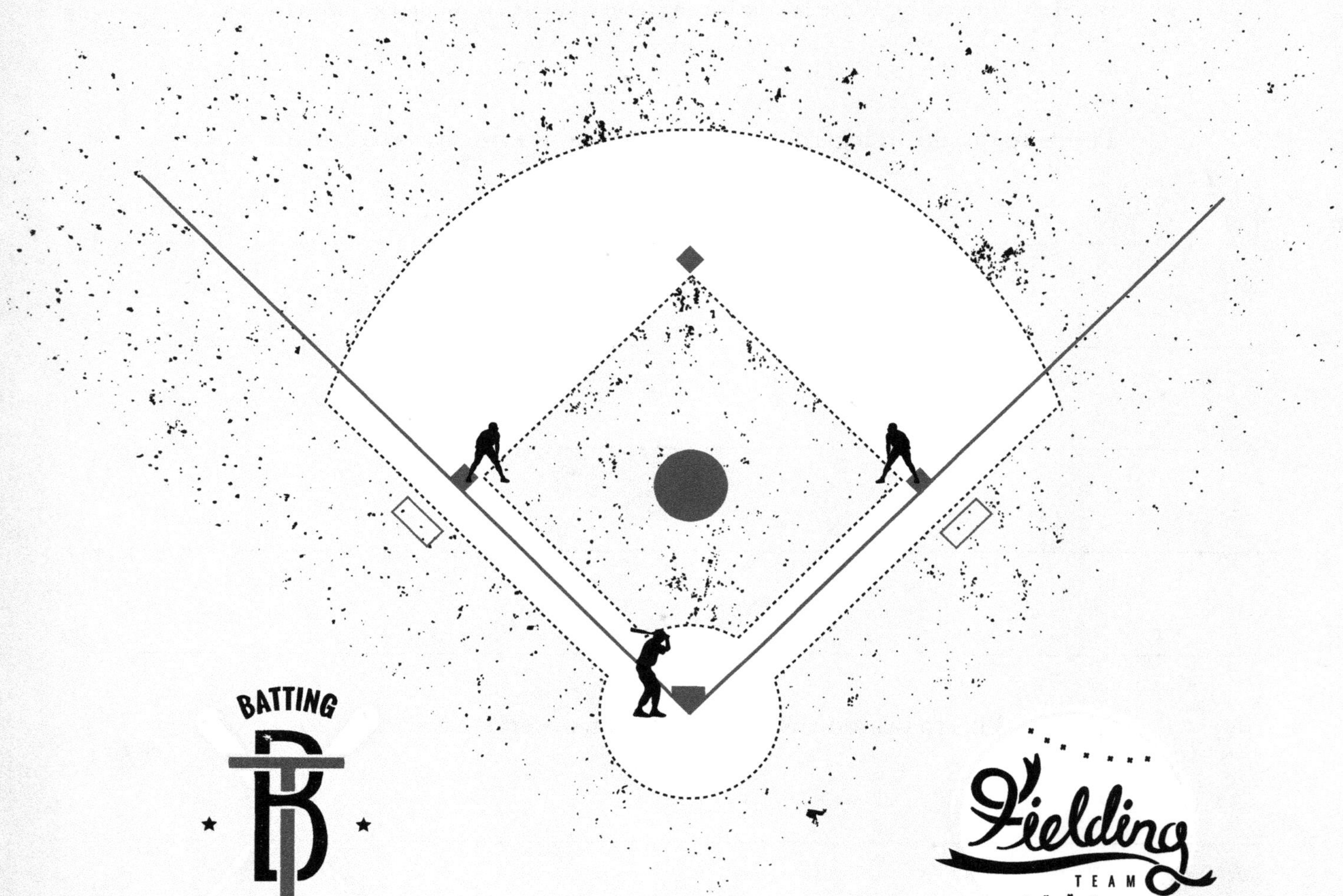

BATTING TEAM

One run scored, runners safe Second and Third	**3** PTS
One run scored, runners safe First and Second	**2** PTS
One run scored (one out)	**1** PT

Fielding Team

3 PTS	One runner on base no run scored (two out)
2 PTS	Two runners on base (one out)
1 PT	Loaded bases.

DOWNLOAD

www.thinkingplayers.com/scenarios/dtp_scenarios_8.pdf

ABOUT SCENARIO EIGHT

Scenario eight occurs early in the game with the fielding team ahead by just one run. With no outs and runners on First and Third the fielding team has to decide whether loading the bases is a better option than getting an out and letting in a run. Would it make a difference if the out was at Second, leaving the runner at First, as compared to getting the out at First and leaving a runner on Second? For the batting team which is the best place to hit the ball? Why?

Points to discuss in regards to tactical decisions made by the teams:

_____

_____

_____

_____

_____

Specific skills to work on as identified from observing the scenarios:

_____

_____

_____

_____

_____

_____

SCORE

SCENARIO	OUTS	FIELDING 9	INNINGS	RUNNERS
9	ONE	BATTING 1	TOP OF SEVEN/FIVE	THIRD

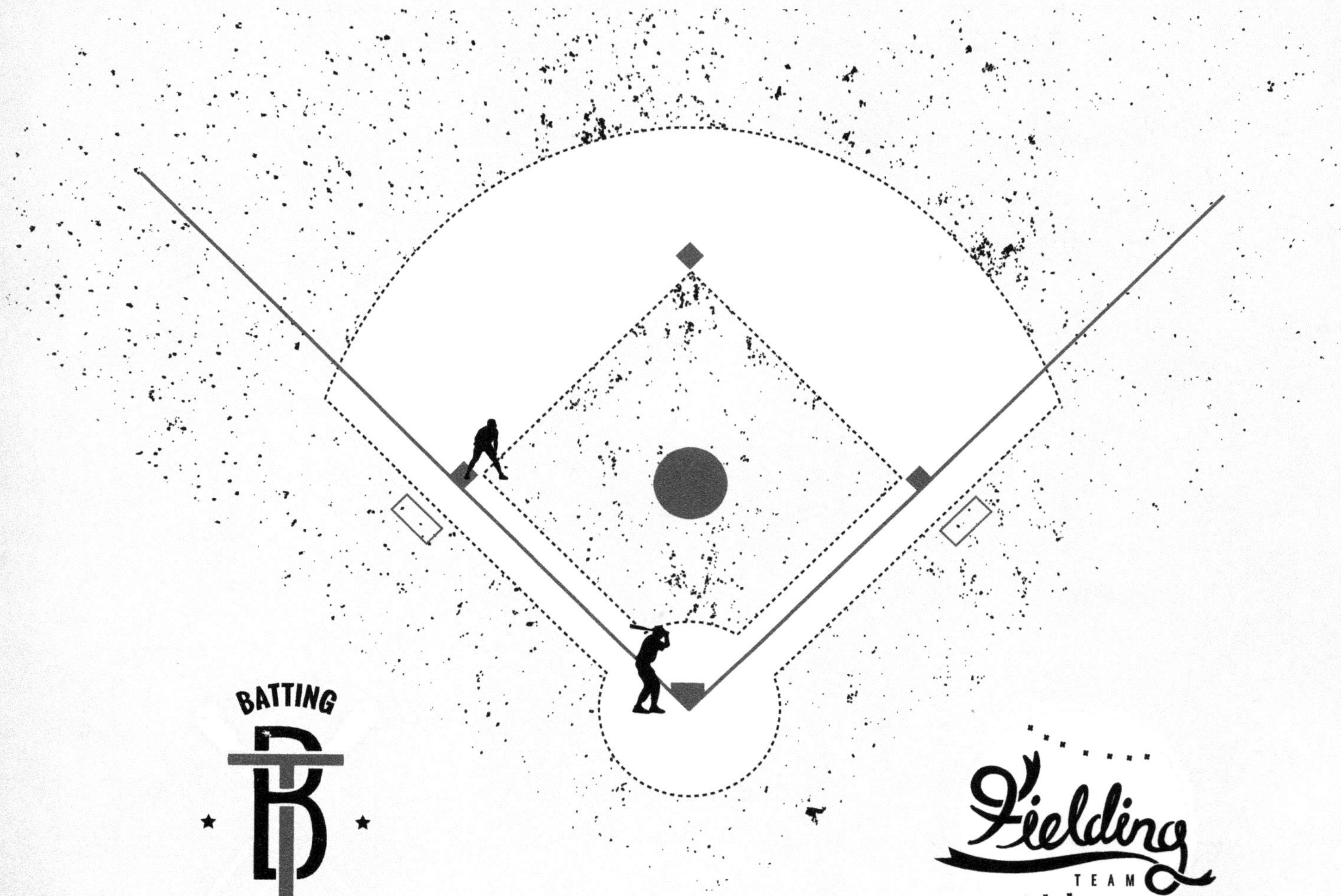

BATTING TEAM

One run scored, runner safe on Second	**3** PTS
One run scored, runner safe on First	**2** PTS
One run scored (two out)	**1** PT

Fielding TEAM

3 PTS	Runner on Third (two out)
2 PTS	One run scored (two out)
1 PT	Runners on First and Second

DOWNLOAD

www.thinkingplayers.com/scenarios/dtp_scenarios_9.pdf

ABOUT SCENARIO NINE

Scenario nine occurs towards the end of the game. With an eight run lead and one out what is the priority tactic for the fielding team. Is the best tactic to concentrate on getting the second out, leaving the runner to score? For the batting team should the priority be getting a second runner on or would sacrificing the batter to score be the best tactic?

Points to discuss in regards to tactical decisions made by the teams:
_____
_____
_____
_____

Specific skills to work on as identified from observing the scenarios:
_____
_____
_____
_____
_____
_____

SCENARIO	OUTS	SCORE	INNINGS	RUNNERS
10	ONE	FIELDING 5 / BATTING 5	TOP OF NINE/SEVEN	NO RUNNERS

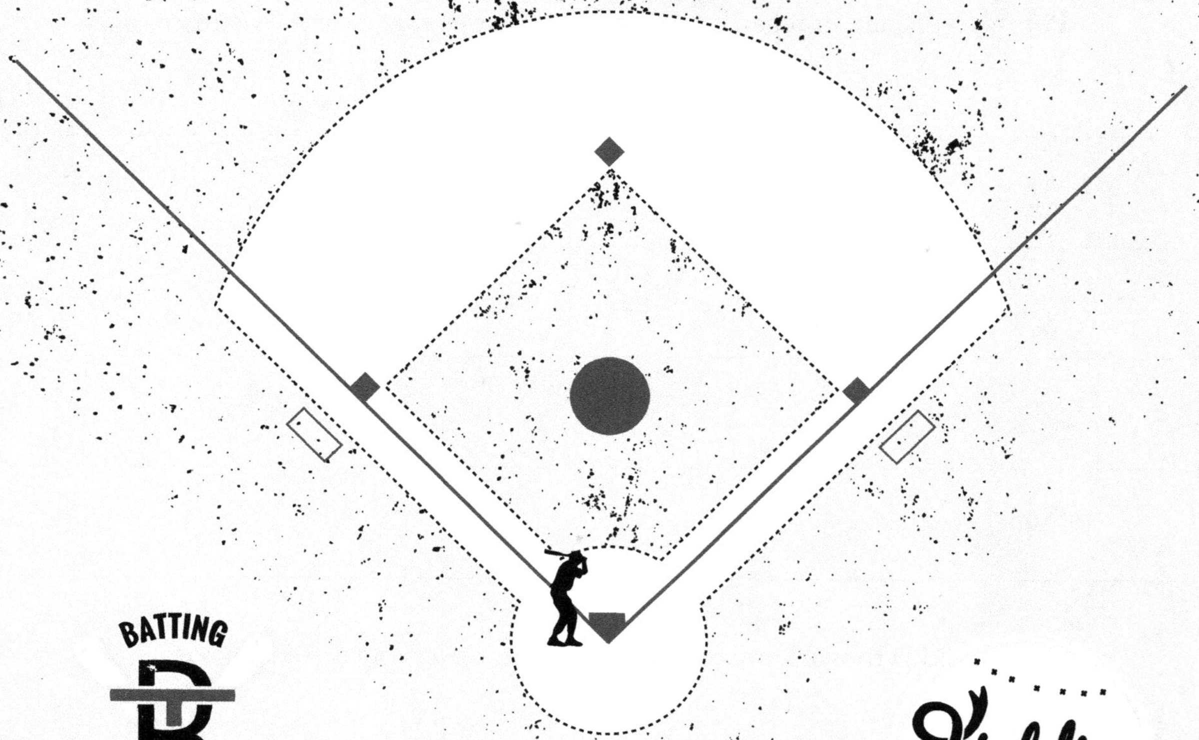

Batting Team

Runner Third or home	**3** PTS
Runner on Second	**2** PTS
Runner on First	**1** PT

Fielding Team

3 PTS	No runner on (two outs)
2 PTS	Runner on First (one out)
1 PT	Runner on Second (one out)

DOWNLOAD

www.thinkingplayers.com/scenarios/dtp_scenarios_10.pdf

ABOUT SCENARIO TEN

Scenario ten occurs in the last innings of a tied game with one out. The game situation puts extra pressure on all players who understand that time is running out to take control of the game. What influence does the game situation have on decision-making, the willingness to take risks and the balance of risk and reward?

Points to discuss in regards to tactical decisions made by the teams:
_____
_____
_____
_____
_____

Specific skills to work on as identified from observing the scenarios:
_____
_____
_____
_____
_____
_____

SCORE

SCENARIO 11	OUTS	FIELDING 3	INNINGS	RUNNERS
	ONE	BATTING 2	TOP OF NINE/SEVEN	SECOND

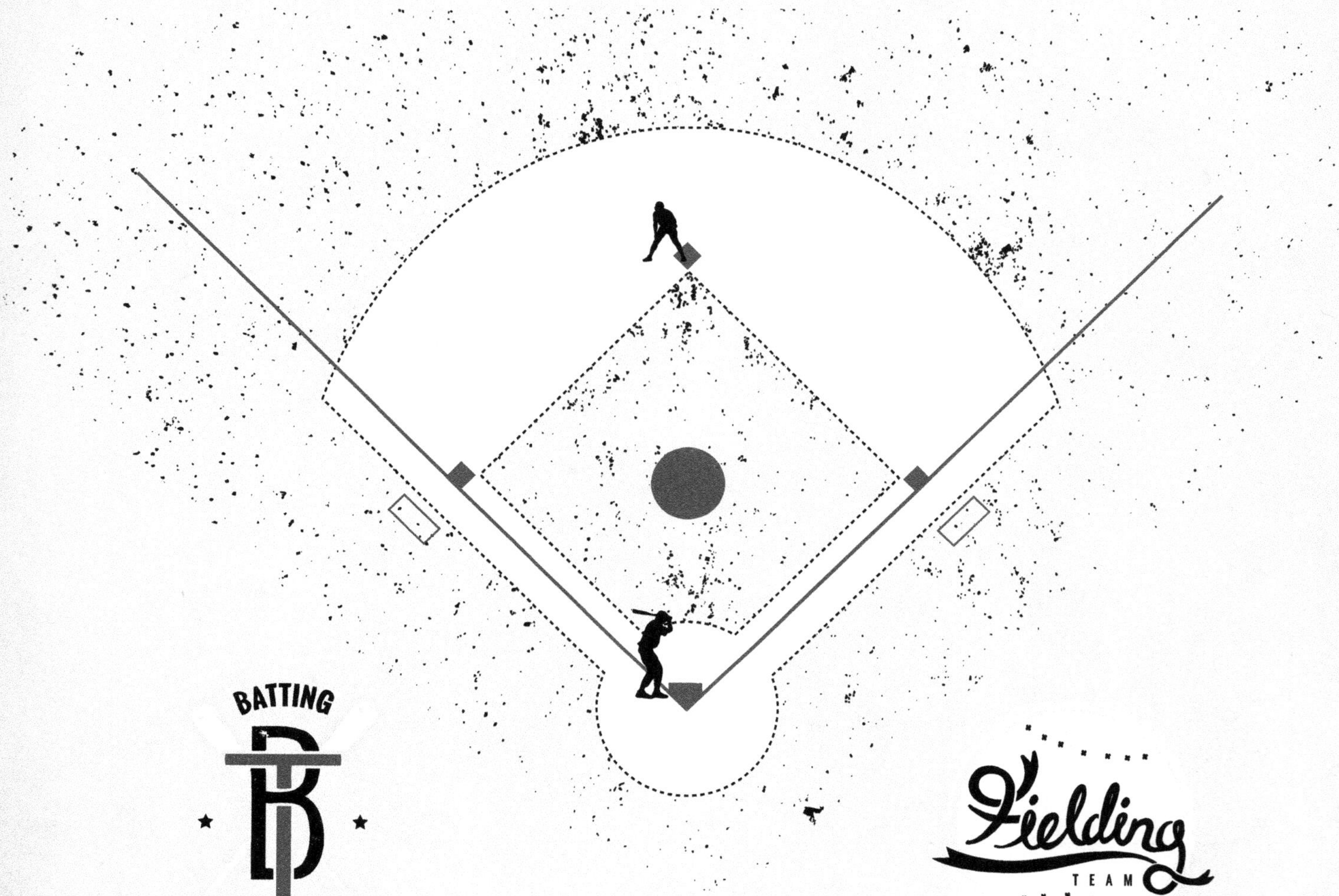

BATTING TEAM

One run scored	**3** PTS
Runners safe Third and First or Second (one out)	**2** PTS
Runner safe on Third (two outs)	**1** PT

Fielding Team

3 PTS	Runner safe on Second (two outs)
2 PTS	Runner safe on First and Second (one out)
1 PT	Runner safe on Third (two outs)

DOWNLOAD

www.thinkingplayers.com/scenarios/dtp_scenarios_11.pdf

ABOUT SCENARIO ELEVEN

Scenario eleven occurs in the last innings of a tight game with the fielding team up by one. The batting team has a runner in scoring position and one out in what is their last turn at bat. What is the number one priority for each team? Will the fielding team having a further turn at bat influence their approach?

Points to discuss in regards to tactical decisions made by the teams:
_____
_____
_____
_____

Specific skills to work on as identified from observing the scenarios:
_____
_____
_____
_____
_____
_____

SCENARIO	OUTS	SCORE	INNINGS	RUNNERS
12	NONE	FIELDING 2 / BATTING 3	TOP OF THREE/TWO	THIRD

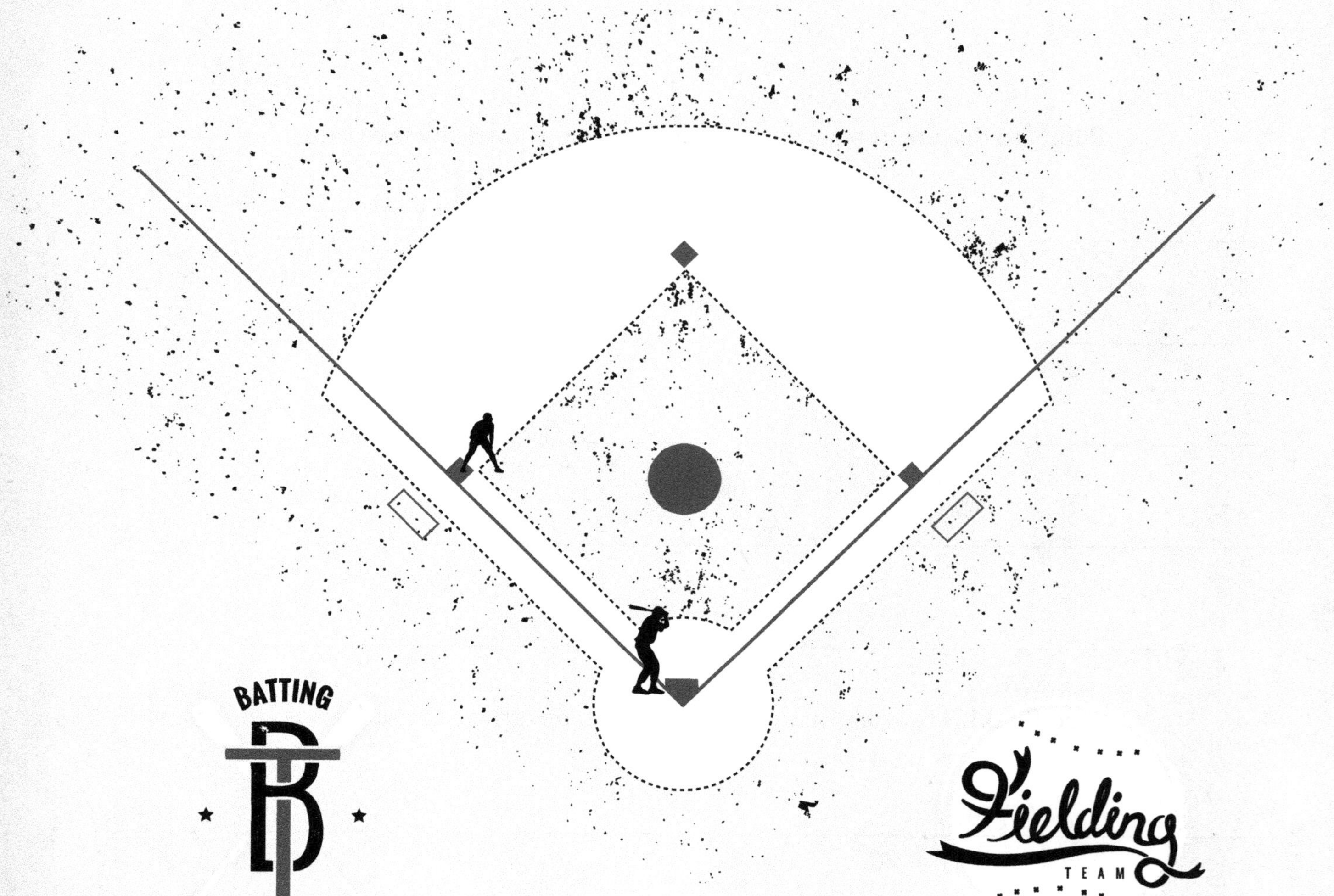

BATTING TEAM

One run scored (no outs)	**3** PTS
One run scored (one out)	**2** PTS
Runners safe Third and First or Second	**1** PT

FIELDING TEAM

3 PTS	No run scored (one out)
2 PTS	No run scored runners safe Third and First
1 PT	No run scored runners safe Third and Second

DOWNLOAD

www.thinkingplayers.com/scenarios/dtp_scenarios_12.pdf

ABOUT SCENARIO TWELVE

Scenario twelve is early in the game with a runner in prime scoring position. No outs places the batting team in a very strong position to score. Where is the best and worst place for the batter to hit? Is it better to have one out and runner scored than having two runners on and still no outs? What should be the priority for the fielding team?

Points to discuss in regards to tactical decisions made by the teams:

_____
_____
_____
_____

Specific skills to work on as identified from observing the scenarios:

_____
_____
_____
_____
_____

SCORE

SCENARIO	OUTS	FIELDING 10	INNINGS	RUNNERS
13	**NONE**	**BATTING 3**	**BOTTOM OF NINE/SEVEN**	**THIRD**

BATTING TEAM

Fielding TEAM

One run scored (none out)	**3** PTS	
One run scored (one out)	**2** PTS	
Runners safe Third and First or Second	**1** PT	

3 PTS	No run scored (one out)	
2 PTS	One run scored (one out)	
1 PT	No run scored, runners safe Third and First	

DOWNLOAD

www.thinkingplayers.com/scenarios/dtp_scenarios_13.pdf

ABOUT SCENARIO THIRTEEN

Scenario thirteen occurs with the batting team well behind and at bat for the final time. Should the fielding team ignore the runner at this stage and simply concentrate on getting the batter out? For the batting team is it better to score the runner and have one out or to have two runners on and no outs? Where should the batter hit?

Points to discuss in regards to tactical decisions made by the teams:
_____
_____
_____
_____
_____

Specific skills to work on as identified from observing the scenarios:
_____
_____
_____
_____
_____
_____

SCORE

SCENARIO 14	OUTS	FIELDING 5	INNINGS	RUNNERS
	ONE	BATTING 4	TOP OF EIGHT/SIX	SECOND & THIRD

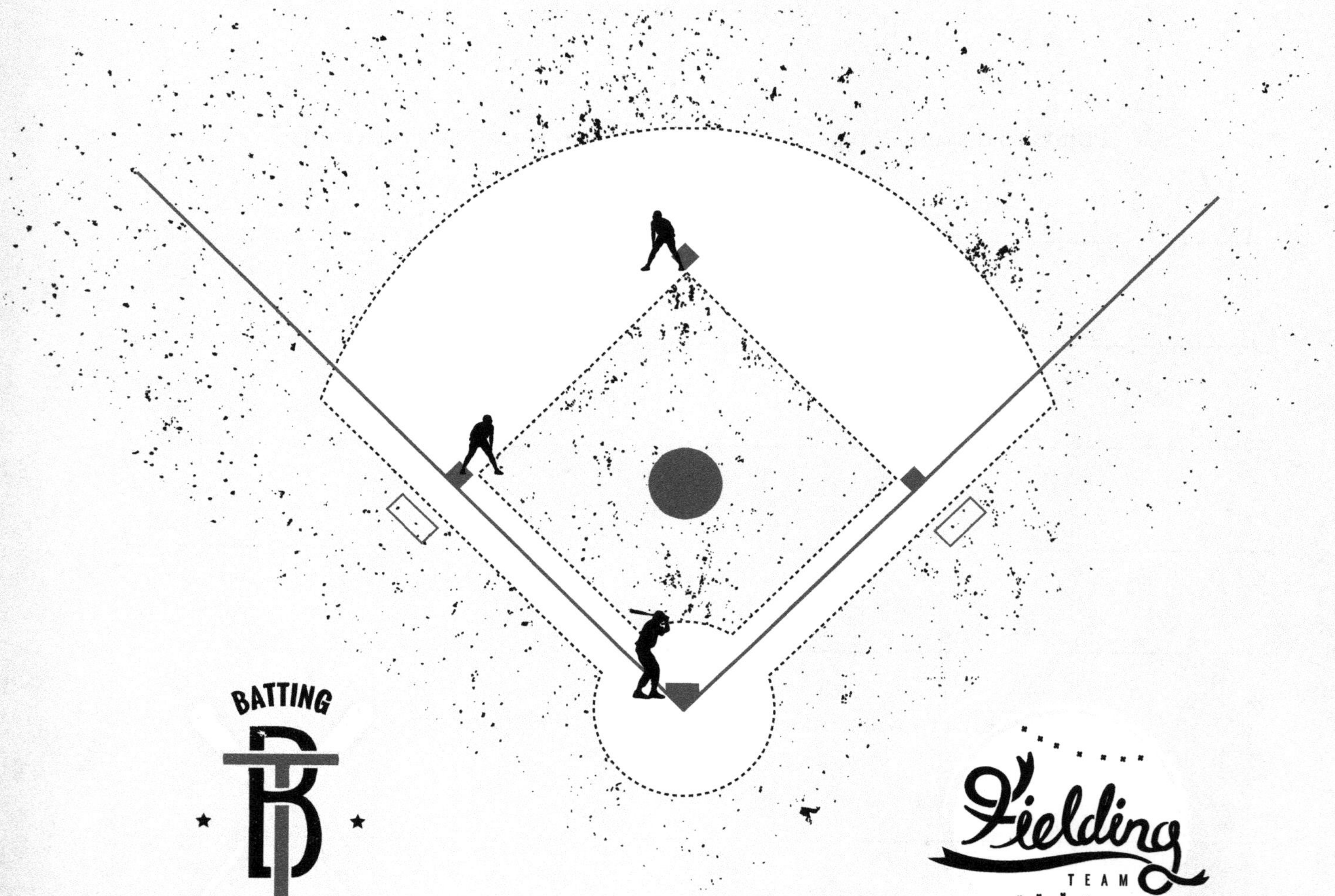

BATTING TEAM

Fielding TEAM

Two runs scored	**3** PTS	
One run scored	**2** PTS	
Runners on First, Second and Third (one out)	**1** PT	

3 PTS	No run scored (two out)
2 PTS	Runners on First, Second and First (one out)
1 PT	One run scored (two outs)

DOWNLOAD

www.thinkingplayers.com/scenarios/dtp_scenarios_14.pdf

ABOUT SCENARIO FOURTEEN

Scenario fourteen occurs in the top of the second to last innings with the fielding teams up by one. With one out, two runners in scoring position and only a force play at First this scenario offers a number of alternative plays. Would loading up the bases be an option at this stage? If so what are the advantages and disadvantages of doing so? What influence does the batting order have on this decision? Is it a good call for the batting team to sacrifice a runner to score a run? How about a squeeze play or a bunt?

Points to discuss in regards to tactical decisions made by the teams:

_____

_____

_____

_____

_____

Specific skills to work on as identified from observing the scenarios:

_____

_____

_____

_____

_____

SCENARIO	OUTS	FIELDING 3	INNINGS	RUNNERS
15	**TWO**	**BATTING 3**	**TOP OF NINE/SEVEN**	**SECOND**

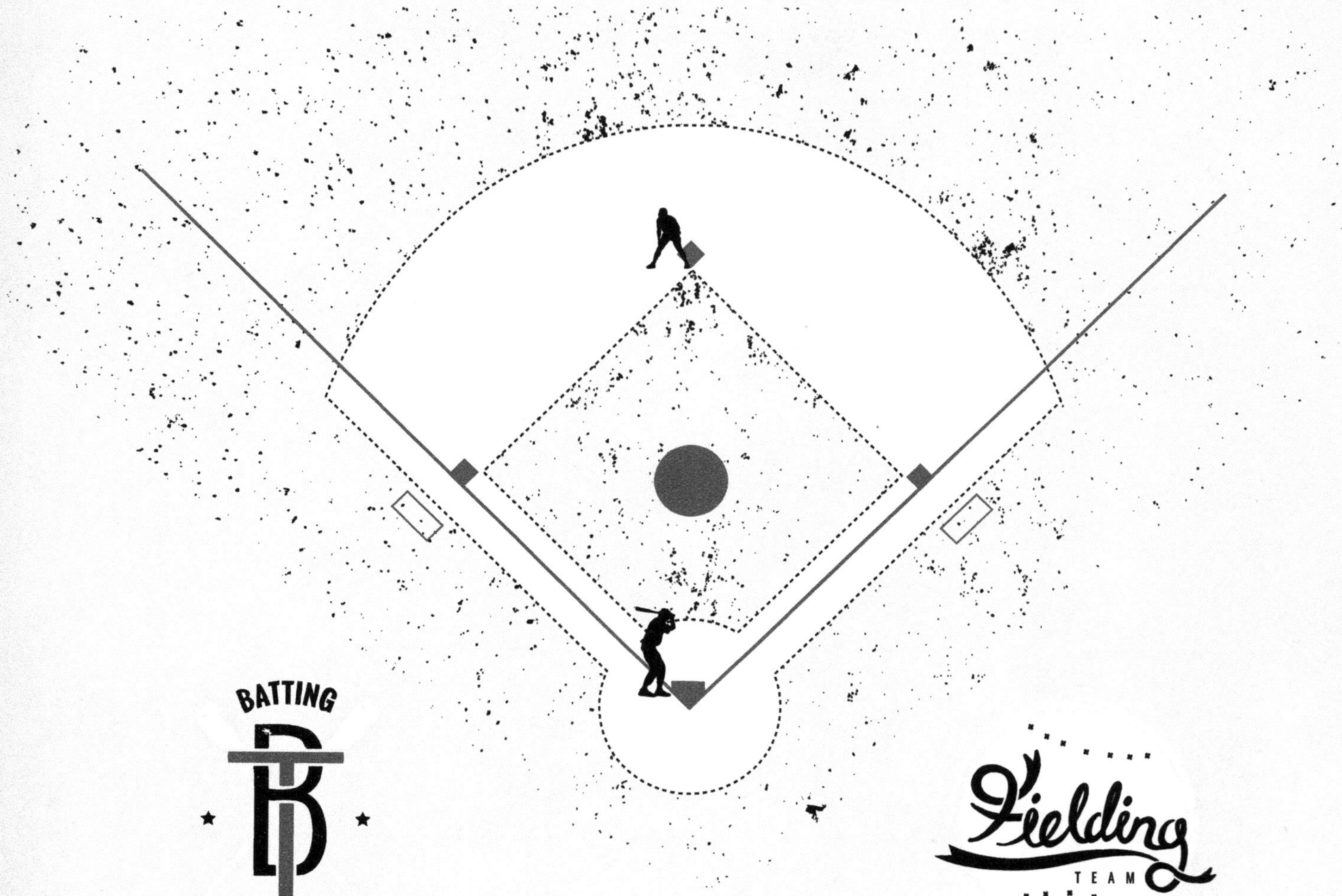

SCORE

BATTING TEAM

One run scored	3 PTS
Runner on Second and Third	2 PTS
Runner on First and Third	1 PT

FIELDING TEAM

3 PTS	Three outs, no run scored
2 PTS	Runner on Second and First
1 PT	Runner on Third and (First or Second)

DOWNLOAD

www.thinkingplayers.com/scenarios/dtp_scenarios_15.pdf

ABOUT SCENARIO FIFTEEN

Scenario fifteen occurs in the top of the last innings with the teams tied. Two outs with a runner in scoring position the batting team has to score a run or at least advance the runner without another out. What can the batting team do to achieve this in what has been a low scoring game? What is the major focus for the fielding team?

Points to discuss in regards to tactical decisions made by the teams:

_____
_____
_____
_____
_____

Specific skills to work on as identified from observing the scenarios:

_____
_____
_____
_____
_____
_____
_____

SCORE

SCENARIO 16	OUTS	FIELDING 7	INNINGS	RUNNERS
	NONE	BATTING 6	TOP OF EIGHT/SIX	FIRST

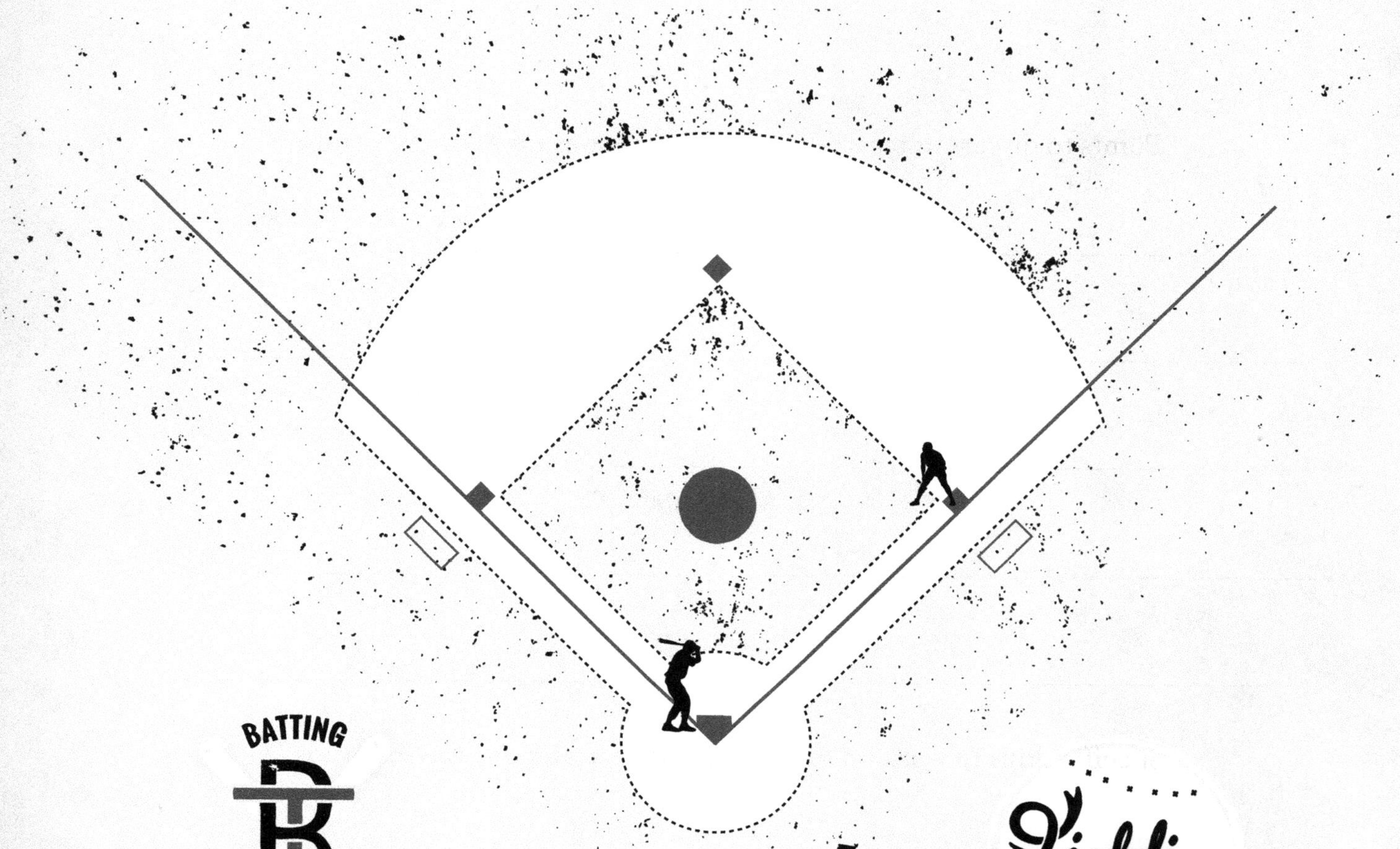

BATTING TEAM

Runner on Third and First or Second (no outs)	**3** PTS
Runner on First and Second (no outs)	**2** PTS
Runner on Second or Third (one out)	**1** PT

FIELDING TEAM

3 PTS	Double Play
2 PTS	Runner on First (one out)
1 PT	Runner on Second (one out)

DOWNLOAD

www.thinkingplayers.com/scenarios/dtp_scenarios_16.pdf

ABOUT SCENARIO SIXTEEN

Scenario sixteen occurs in the top of the second to last innings with no outs and a runner on First. This is a fairly standard situation that teams will face on many occasions. What is the major focus for the fielding and batting teams?

Points to discuss in regards to tactical decisions made by the teams:
___
___
___
___
___

Specific skills to work on as identified from observing the scenarios:
___
___
___
___
___
___

SCENARIO 17	OUTS	FIELDING 7	INNINGS	RUNNERS
		SCORE		
	NONE	BATTING 1	BOTTOM OF FOUR/THREE	SECOND

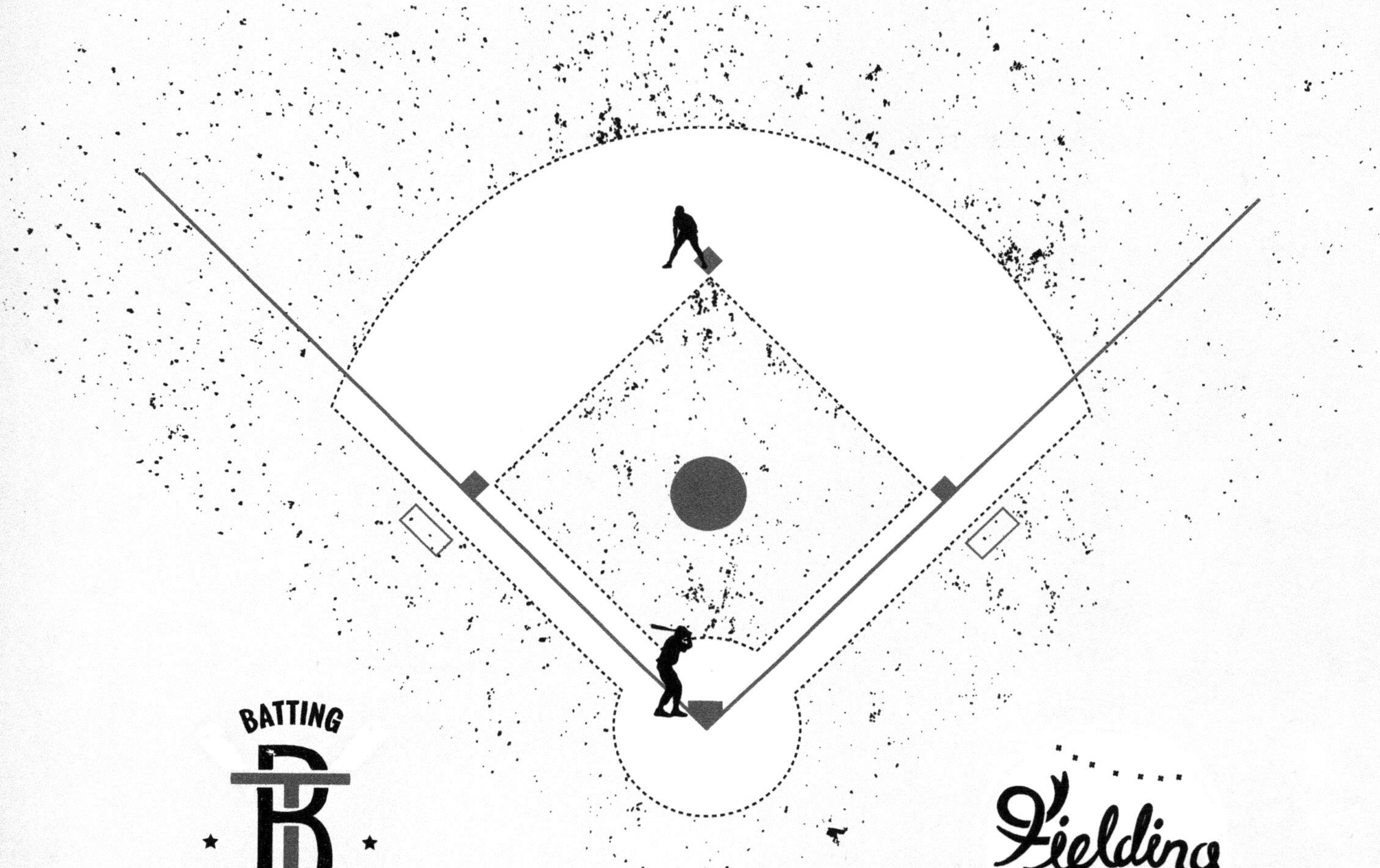

BATTING TEAM

Fielding TEAM

One run scored (no outs)	**3** PTS	
One run scored (one out)	**2** PTS	
No run scored (no outs)	**1** PT	

3 PTS	Runner on Second (one out)	
2 PTS	Runner on Third (one out)	
1 PT	Runners on First and Third (no outs)	

DOWNLOAD

www.thinkingplayers.com/scenarios/dtp_scenarios_17.pdf

ABOUT SCENARIO SEVENTEEN

Scenario seventeen occurs in middle phase of the game with the fielding team having established a solid lead. The batting team has a runner in scoring position and no outs. How important is it for the fielding team to hold the runner at Second in comparison to getting the out? Is it a better for the fielding team to have runners on First and Second with no outs or a runner on Third with one out? What about for the batting team? Where should the batter be trying to hit the ball in this situation?

Points to discuss in regards to tactical decisions made by the teams:

_____
_____
_____
_____

Specific skills to work on as identified from observing the scenarios:

_____
_____
_____
_____

SCORE

SCENARIO 18	OUTS	FIELDING 5	INNINGS	RUNNERS
	ONE	BATTING 5	BOTTOM OF NINE/SEVEN	THIRD

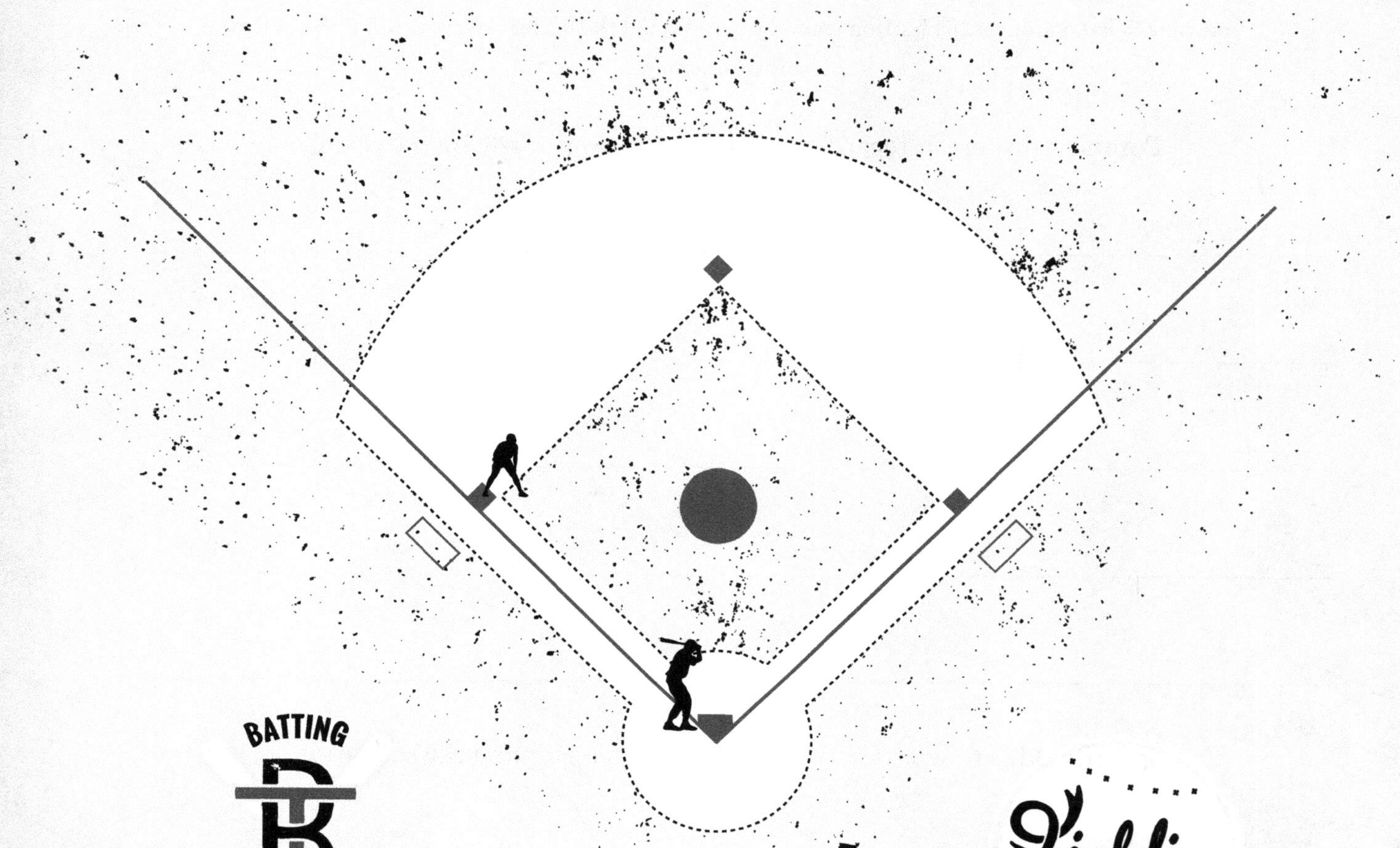

BATTING TEAM

Fielding TEAM

One run scored	**3** PTS	
Runners on Second and Third (one out)	**2** PTS	
Runners on First and Third (one out)	**1** PT	

3 PTS	No Run Scores (two outs)	
2 PTS	Runners on First and Third (one out)	
1 PT	Runners on Second and Third (one out)	

DOWNLOAD

www.thinkingplayers.com/scenarios/dtp_scenarios_18.pdf

ABOUT SCENARIO EIGHTEEN

Scenario eighteen occurs in the last turn at bat in a tied ball game with one out and a runner on Third. This is a pressure position with both teams knowing that a scored run ends the game. Where should the fielding team position themselves? What is their focus and how important is getting the second out? Is it worth risking a scored run by throwing to First, for example? How important at this point is where in the batting order are the next batters coming from. What are the positives and negatives of walking the batter?

Points to discuss in regards to tactical decisions made by the teams:

_____
_____
_____
_____
_____

Specific skills to work on as identified from observing the scenarios:

_____
_____
_____
_____
_____

SCORE

SCENARIO	OUTS	FIELDING 1	INNINGS	RUNNERS
19	**NONE**	**BATTING 1**	**BOTTOM OF SEVEN/FIVE**	**FIRST & SECOND**

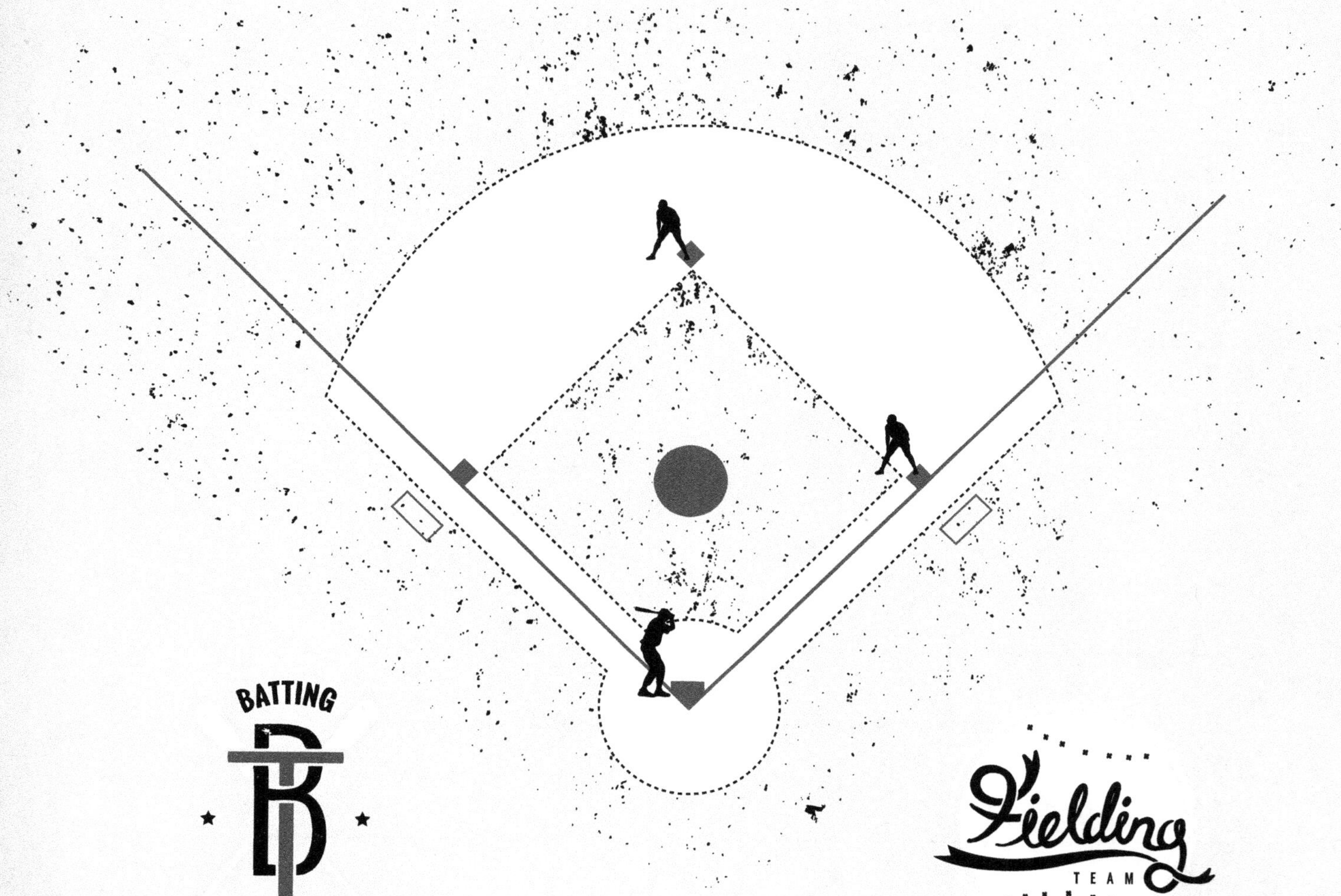

BATTING TEAM

Fielding TEAM

One or more runs scored (no outs)	**3** PTS	
One run scored (one out)	**2** PTS	
Bases Loaded (no outs)	**1** PT	

3 PTS	No run scores, Double Play (two outs)
2 PTS	Runners on First and Second (one out)
1 PT	Bases Loaded (no outs)

DOWNLOAD

www.thinkingplayers.com/scenarios/dtp_scenarios_19.pdf

ABOUT SCENARIO NINETEEN

Scenario nineteen occurs in the bottom of seven/five of a low scoring game with the score tied and no outs. The fielding team has a force play at First, Second and Third with good opportunities for double plays. The batting team has to consider how to avoid this while advancing and hopefully scoring runners.

Points to discuss in regards to tactical decisions made by the teams:

_____
_____
_____
_____
_____

Specific skills to work on as identified from observing the scenarios:

_____
_____
_____
_____
_____
_____

SCORE

SCENARIO 20	OUTS	FIELDING 0	INNINGS	RUNNERS
	NONE	BATTING 5	BOTTOM OF SIX/FOUR	SECOND & THIRD

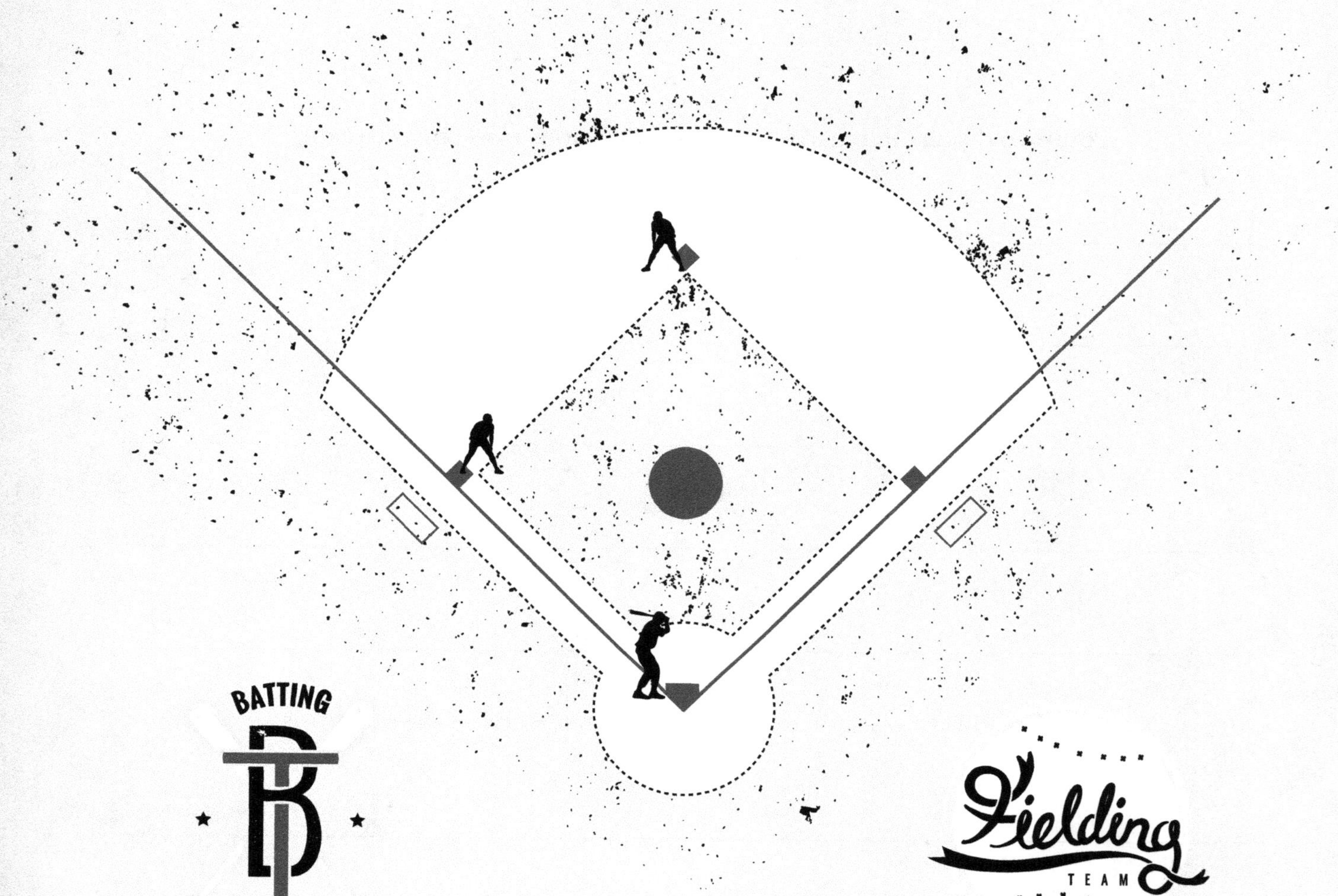

BATTING TEAM

Fielding TEAM

Two runs scored (no outs)	3 PTS
Two runs scored (one out)	2 PTS
One run scored (no outs)	1 PT

3 PTS	No run scores (one out)
2 PTS	Bases loaded (no outs)
1 PT	One run scored (one out)

DOWNLOAD

www.thinkingplayers.com/scenarios/dtp_scenarios_20.pdf

ABOUT SCENARIO TWENTY

Scenario twenty occurs in the bottom of the sixth/fourth with two runners in scoring position and no outs. The batting team has established a strong lead but will be aware there is still a lot of the game to go. They will be looking to move further ahead in an attempt to make the game more secure. The fielding team is under pressure to minimize any further damage. What is their major emphasis and how will they react tactically? What are their options in regards to preventing more runs?

Points to discuss in regards to tactical decisions made by the teams:

_____
_____
_____
_____

Specific skills to work on as identified from observing the scenarios:

_____
_____
_____
_____
_____
_____

SCORE

SCENARIO 21	OUTS	FIELDING 3	INNINGS	RUNNERS
	TWO	BATTING 2	BOTTOM OF FIVE/FOUR	FIRST & SECOND

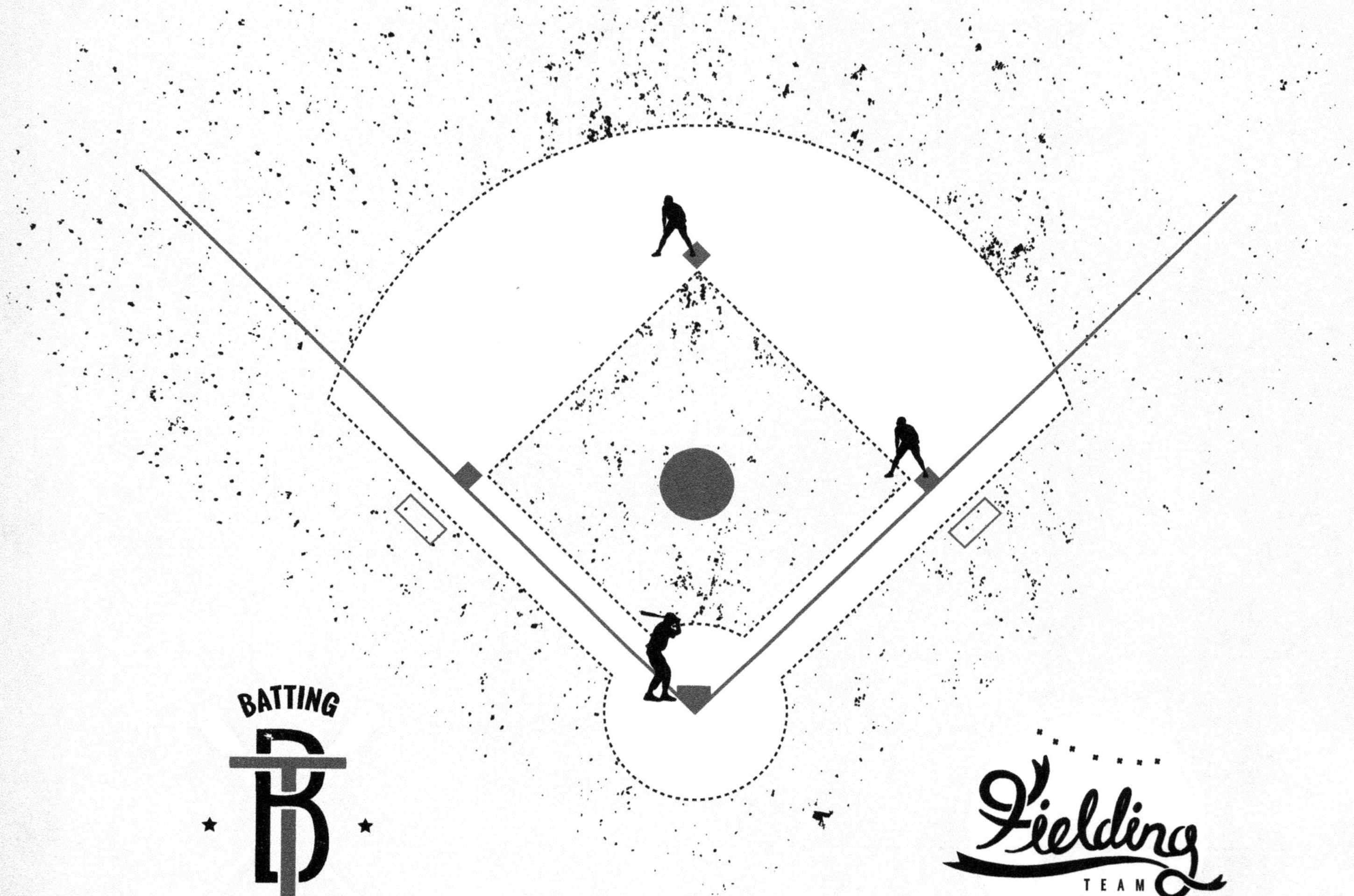

BATTING TEAM

Fielding TEAM

Two runs scored (two outs)	3 PTS
One run scored (two outs)	2 PTS
Bases loaded (two outs)	1 PT

3 PTS	No run scored (three outs)
2 PTS	Bases loaded (two outs)
1 PT	One run scored then third out taken

DOWNLOAD

www.thinkingplayers.com/scenarios/dtp_scenarios_21.pdf

ABOUT SCENARIO TWENTY-ONE

Scenario twenty-one occurs in the middle segment of a tight game with the innings balanced between the two teams. The fielding team only needs one out while the batting team has two runners on including one in scoring position. Where would the best place for the batter to hit the ball be? Would a double steal be a good move at this point? What else could the batting team do to put additional pressure on the fielders?

Points to discuss in regards to tactical decisions made by the teams:

_____
_____
_____
_____
_____

Specific skills to work on as identified from observing the scenarios:

_____
_____
_____
_____
_____
_____

SCORE

SCENARIO 22	OUTS NONE	FIELDING 3 BATTING 4	INNINGS BOTTOM OF SEVEN/FIVE	RUNNERS SECOND

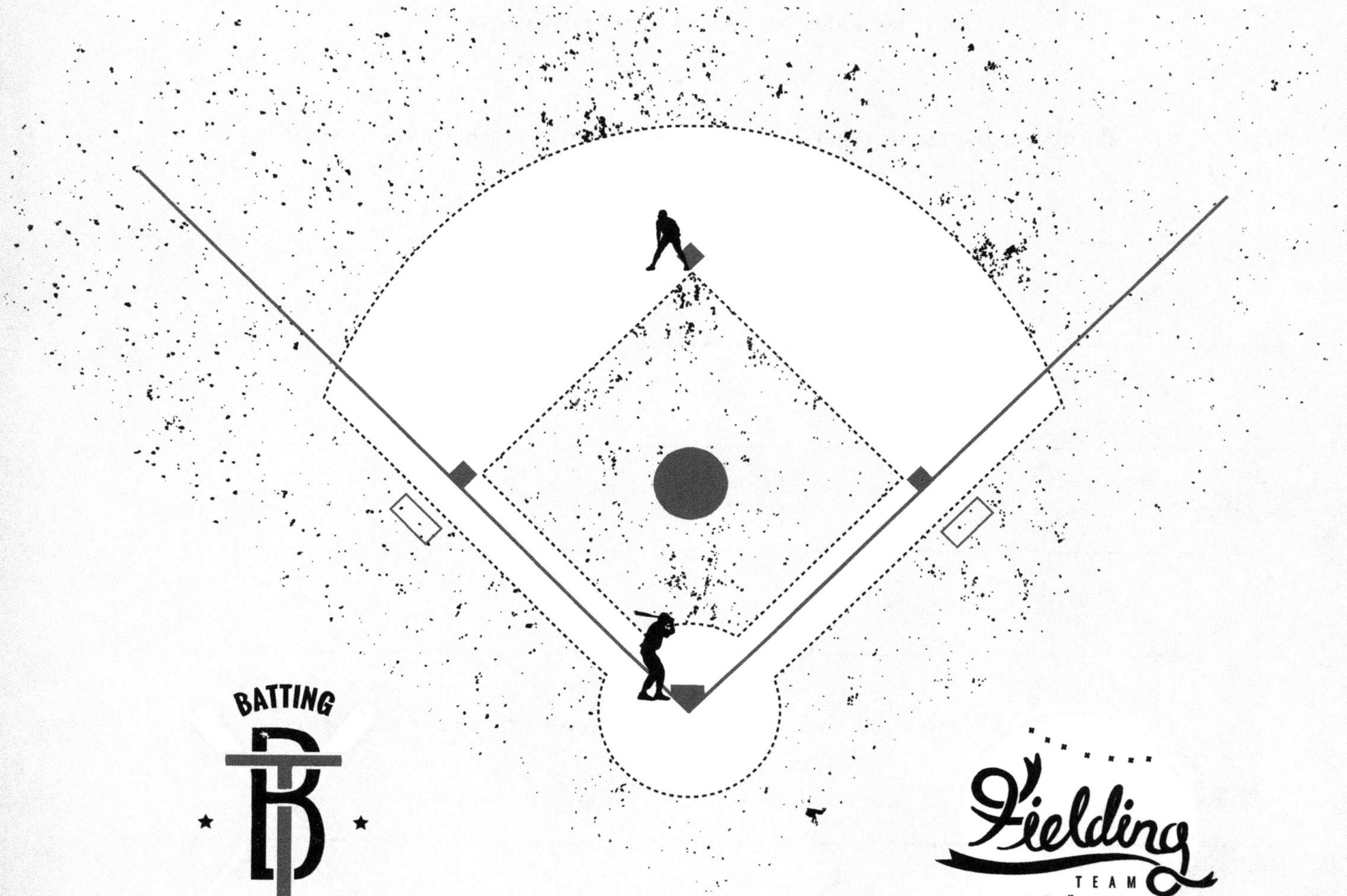

BATTING TEAM

Fielding TEAM

One run scored (no outs)	**3** PTS	
One run scored (one out)	**2** PTS	
Runners on First and Third (no outs)	**1** PT	

3 PTS	Runner on Second (one out)	
2 PTS	Runner on Third (one out)	
1 PT	Runners on First and Second or Third (no outs)	

DOWNLOAD

www.thinkingplayers.com/scenarios/dtp_scenarios_22.pdf

ABOUT SCENARIO TWENTY-TWO

Scenario twenty-two occurs in the bottom of the seventh/fifth innings with the batting team up by one run. With none out and a runner in scoring position the batting team needs to move the runner and hopefully score them. The fielding team needs an out and if possible also hold the runner at Second. Where is the best and worst place for the batter to hit? Is it better for the fielding team to have runners on First and Second and no outs or a runner on Third and one out?

Points to discuss in regards to tactical decisions made by the teams:

_____
_____
_____
_____
_____

Specific skills to work on as identified from observing the scenarios:

_____
_____
_____
_____
_____
_____
_____

SCORE

SCENARIO	OUTS	FIELDING 6	INNINGS	RUNNERS
23	**ONE**	**BATTING 3**	**BOTTOM OF SEVEN/FIVE**	**FIRST & SECOND**

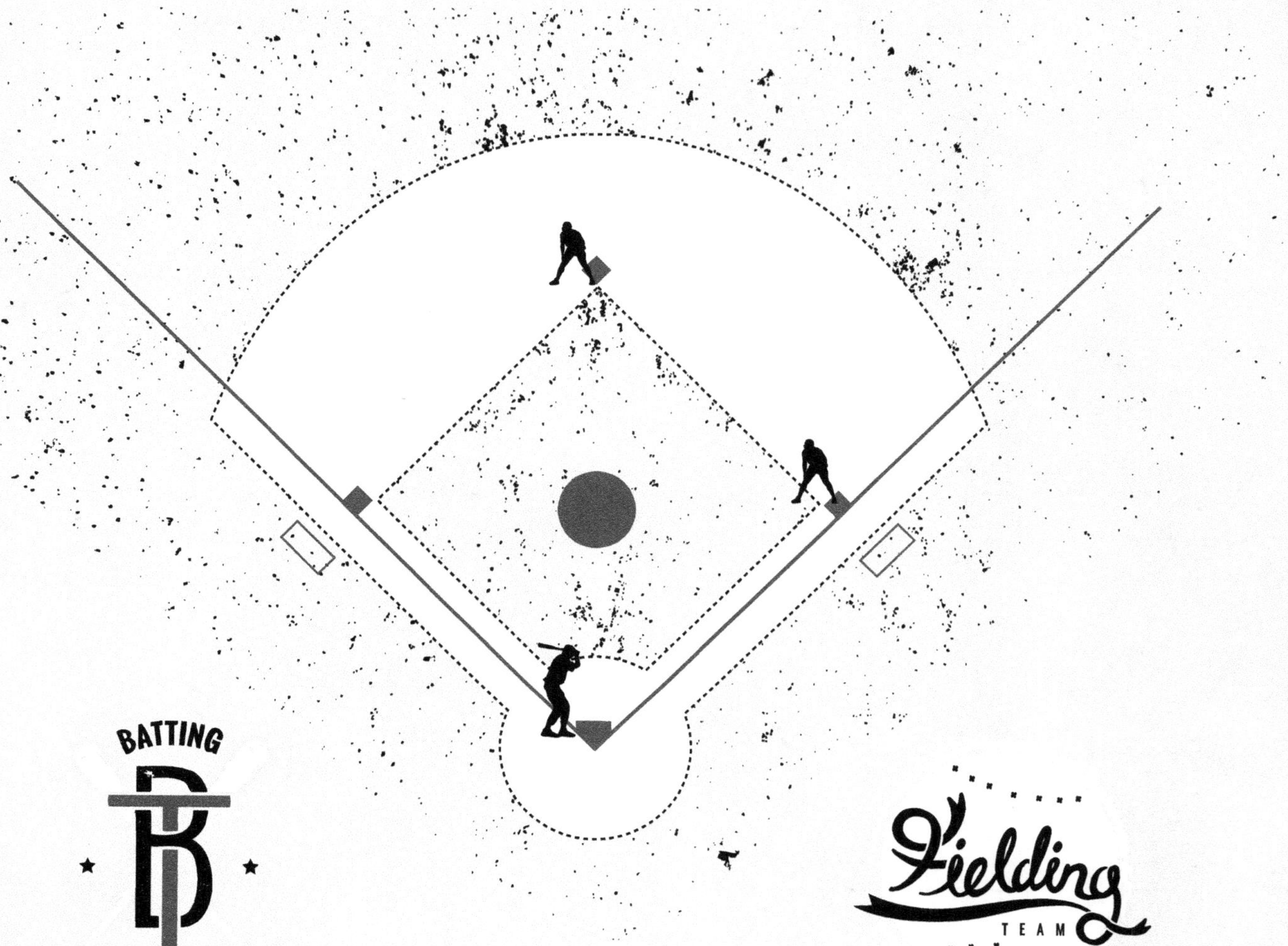

BATTING TEAM

One or two runs scored (one out)	**3** PTS
One or two runs scored (two outs)	**2** PTS
Bases Loaded (one out)	**1** PT

FIELDING TEAM

3 PTS	No run scores (three outs)
2 PTS	Runners on First and Second (two outs)
1 PT	Bases Loaded (one out)

DOWNLOAD

www.thinkingplayers.com/scenarios/dtp_scenarios_23.pdf

ABOUT SCENARIO TWENTY-THREE

Scenario twenty-three occurs in the bottom of the seventh/fifth with runners on First and Second and one out. The batting team has the tying run at bat and only one out so will be looking to move runners and hopefully score. Where should they be looking to hit the ball? What would be the worst place for the batter to hit? For the fielding team what is most important, the second out or stopping the run being scored. If this play ended in loaded bases and one out would that be a positive or negative outcome for the fielding team?

Points to discuss in regards to tactical decisions made by the teams:

_____
_____
_____
_____
_____

Specific skills to work on as identified from observing the scenarios:

_____
_____
_____
_____
_____
_____

SCORE

SCENARIO	OUTS	FIELDING 8	INNINGS	RUNNERS
24	**NONE**	**BATTING 5**	**BOTTOM OF NINE/SEVEN**	**SECOND**

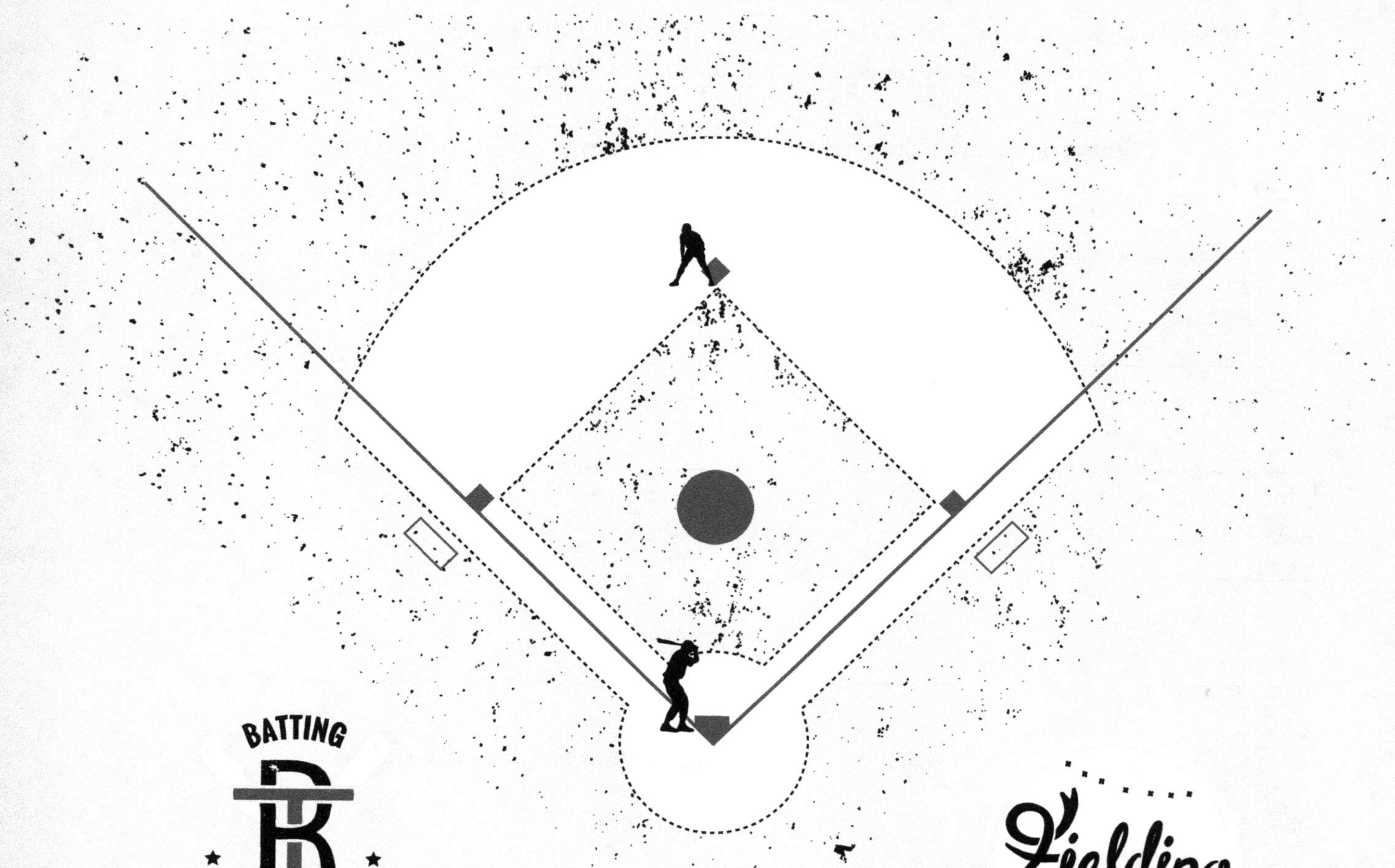

One run scored (no outs)	**3** PTS	**3** PTS	Runner on Second (one out)
One run scored (one out)	**2** PTS	**2** PTS	Runner on Third (one out)
Runners safe on Third and First or Second (no outs)	**1** PT	**1** PT	Runners on First and Third (no outs)

DOWNLOAD

www.thinkingplayers.com/scenarios/dtp_scenarios_24.pdf

ABOUT SCENARIO TWENTY-FOUR

Scenario twenty-four occurs in the bottom of the ninth/seventh with no outs and the fielding team up by three. With a runner on Second how much emphasis should the fielding team put into stopping the run as opposed to getting an out. Should an out at Third be attempted if the opportunity arose or should the fielder choose the out at First and leave the front-runner? Where should the batter be hitting?

Points to discuss in regards to tactical decisions made by the teams:

_____

_____

_____

_____

Specific skills to work on as identified from observing the scenarios:

_____

_____

_____

_____

_____

_____

SCENARIO	OUTS	FIELDING 3	INNINGS	RUNNERS
25		**SCORE**		
	TWO	BATTING 3	BOTTOM OF NINE/SEVEN	THIRD

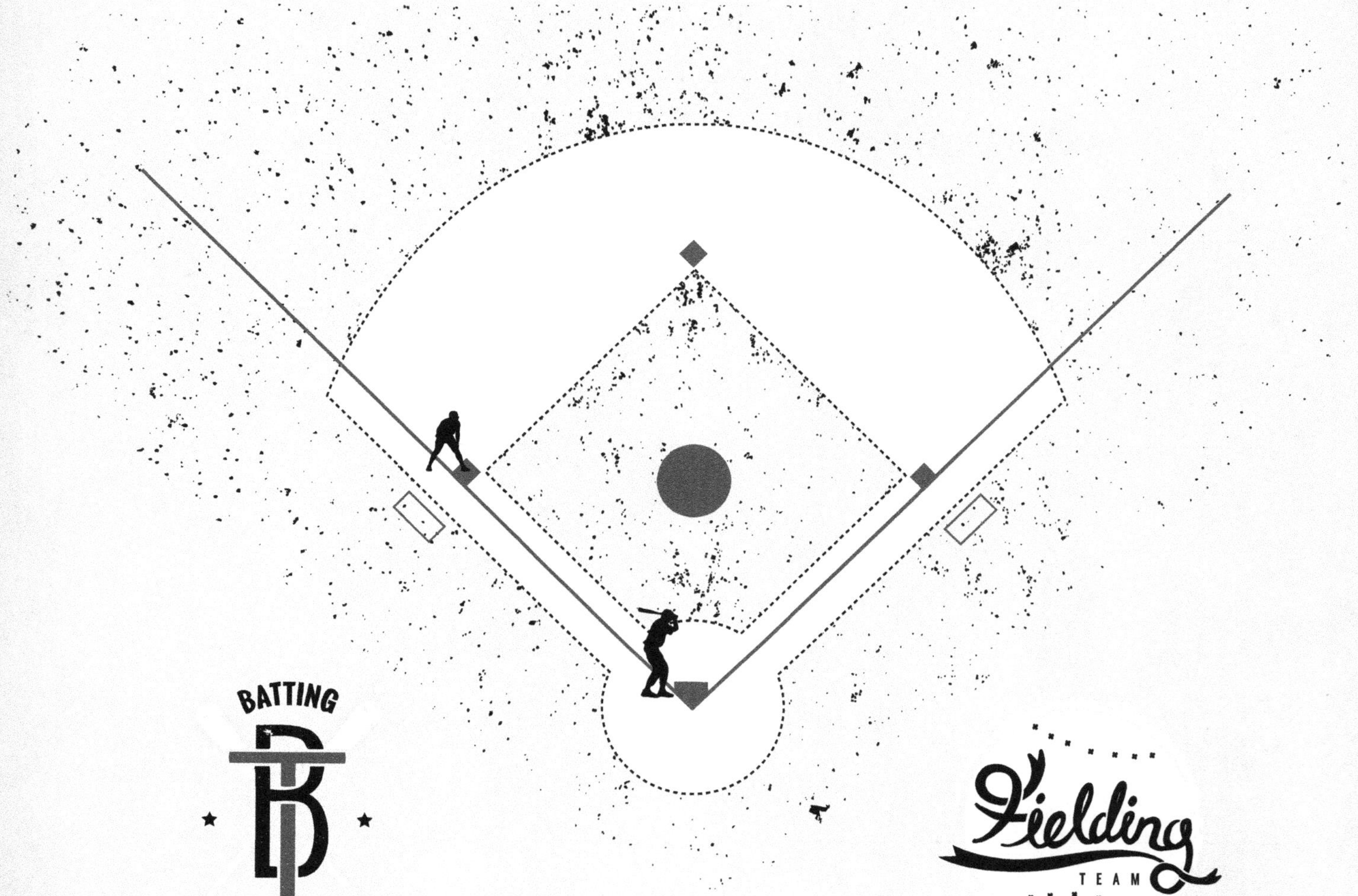

BATTING TEAM

Fielding TEAM

One run scored	**3** PTS	
Runner on Second and Third (two outs)	**2** PTS	
Runner on First and Third (two outs)	**1** PT	

3 PTS	Three outs	
2 PTS	Runners on First and Third	
1 PT	Runners on Second and Third	

DOWNLOAD

www.thinkingplayers.com/scenarios/dtp_scenarios_25.pdf

ABOUT SCENARIO TWENTY-FIVE

Scenario twenty-five occurs in a tied game with two outs and the winning run on Third. This play will decide whether the game is won by the batting team or will go into extra time. For the fielding team the major focus has to be to stop the run scoring and if possible get the third out? Should they field in close or remain in their normal positions? At what point do the fielding team let the runner get to one without a play in order to ensure no run is scored? Where is the best place for the batter to hit considering the need to score the runner but not get an out?

Points to discuss in regards to tactical decisions made by the teams:

_____
_____
_____
_____

Specific skills to work on as identified from observing the scenarios:

_____
_____
_____
_____
_____

OVERVIEW OF SCENARIOS

Scenario Number	Number of Outs	Runner(s)	Score	Innings	QR
One	One	Second	4 (F) - 3 (B)	Top of Six/Five	
Two	Two	First	3 (F) - 3 (B)	Bottom of Five/Four	
Three	Two	First	5 (F) - 4 (B)	Bottom of Nine/Seven	
Four	One	Loaded Bases	4 (F) – 5 (B)	Top of Five/Four	
Five	One	First & Third	10 (F) – 3 (B)	Bottom of Eight/Six	
Six	Two	Second & Third	2 (F) – 2 (B)	Top of Four/Three	
Seven	None	Loaded Bases	7 (F) – 1 (B)	Bottom of Eight/Six	
Eight	None	First & Third	2 (F) – 3 (B)	Bottom of Three/Two	
Nine	One	Third	9 (F) – 1 (B)	Top of Seven/Five	
Ten	One	No Runners	5 (F) – 5 (B)	Top of Nine/Seven	
Eleven	One	Second	3 (F) – 2 (B)	Top of Nine/Seven	
Twelve	None	Third	2 (F) – 3 (B)	Top of Three/Two	
Thirteen	None	Third	10 (F) – 3 (B)	Bottom of Nine/Seven	

Scenario Number	Number of Outs	Runner(s)	Score	Innings	QR
Fourteen	One	Second & Third	5 (F) – 4 (B)	Top of Eight/Six	
Fifteen	Two	Second	3 (F) – 3 (B)	Top of Nine/Seven	
Sixteen	None	First	7 (F) – 6 (B)	Top of Eight/Six	
Seventeen	None	Second	7 (F) – 1 (B)	Bottom of Four/Three	
Eighteen	One	Third	5 (F) – 5 (B)	Bottom of Nine/Seven	
Nineteen	None	First & Second	1 (F) – 1 (B)	Bottom of Seven/Five	
Twenty	None	Second & Third	0 (F) – 5 (B)	Bottom of Six/Four	
Twenty One	Two	First & Second	3 (F) – 2 (B)	Bottom of Five/Four	
Twenty Two	None	Second	3 (F) – 4 (B)	Bottom of Seven/Five	
Twenty Three	One	First & Second	6 (F) – 3 (B)	Bottom of Seven/Five	
Twenty Four	None	Second	8 (F) – 5 (B)	Bottom of Nine/Seven	
Twenty Five	Two	Third	3 (F) – 3 (B)	Bottom of Nine/Seven	

DEVELOPING YOUR OWN
SCENARIOS

This sections contains ten empty templates that you can use to develop your own scenarios. These could be developed as a result of a specific situation that occurred in a game that you would like to revisit or simply an area that you are interested in. The process of developing three, two and one point outcomes could involve the players or be created by you.

An alternative use of these templates could be to give them to the players to develop for a subsequent practice. Again this cognitive engagement will help generate the deeper levels of learning that are so important to understanding the game.

Blank scenario can also be downloaded at.

WWW.THINKINGPLAYERS.COM/SCENARIOS

SCORE

OUTS	FIELDING	INNINGS	RUNNERS
	BATTING		

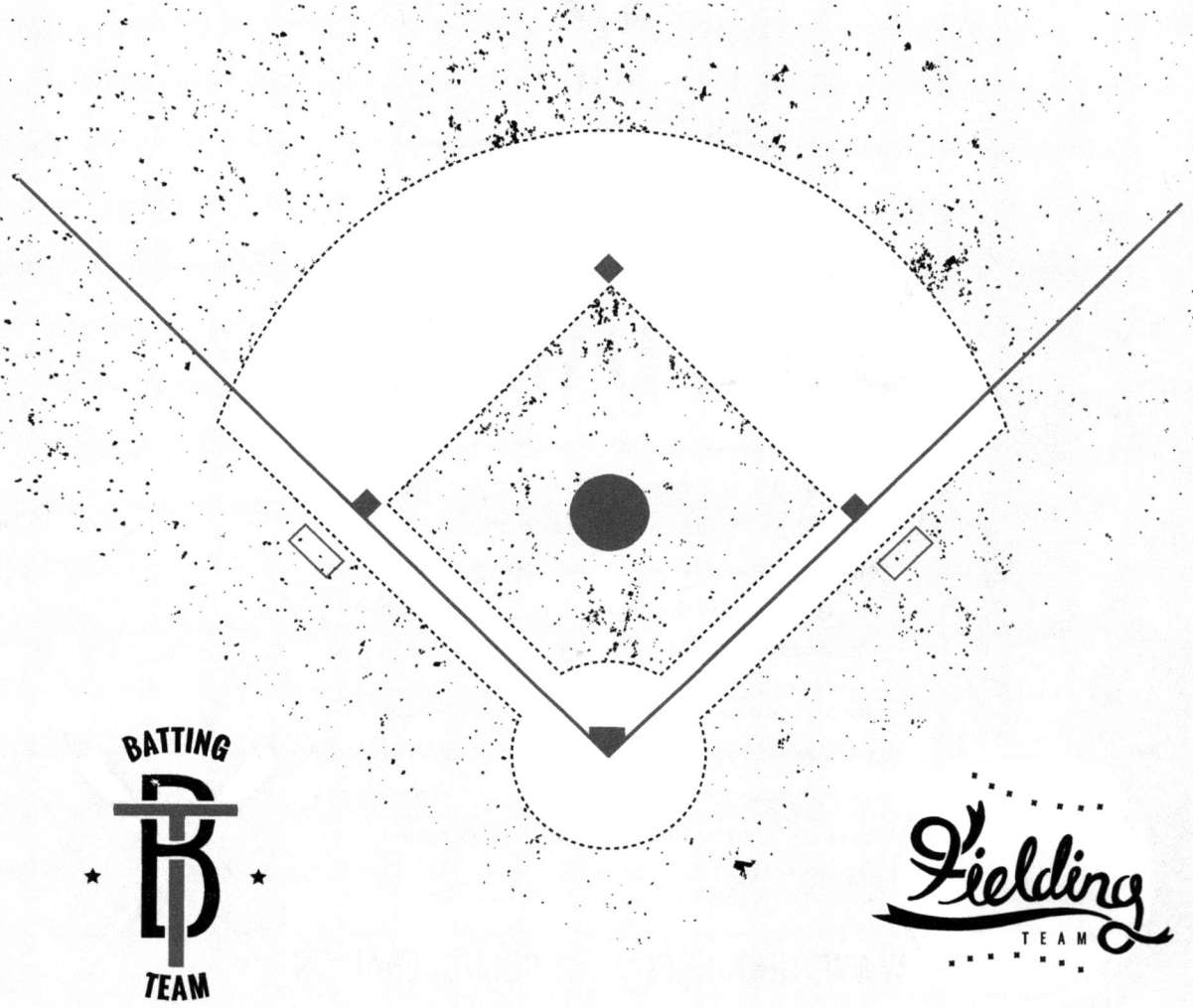

	3 PTS		3 PTS
	2 PTS		2 PTS
	1 PT		1 PT

SCENARIO:

_____

_____

_____

_____

Points to discuss in regards to tactical decisions made by the teams:

_____

_____

_____

_____

_____

Specific skills to work on as identified from observing the scenarios:

_____

_____

_____

_____

_____

SCORE

OUTS	FIELDING	INNINGS	RUNNERS
	BATTING		

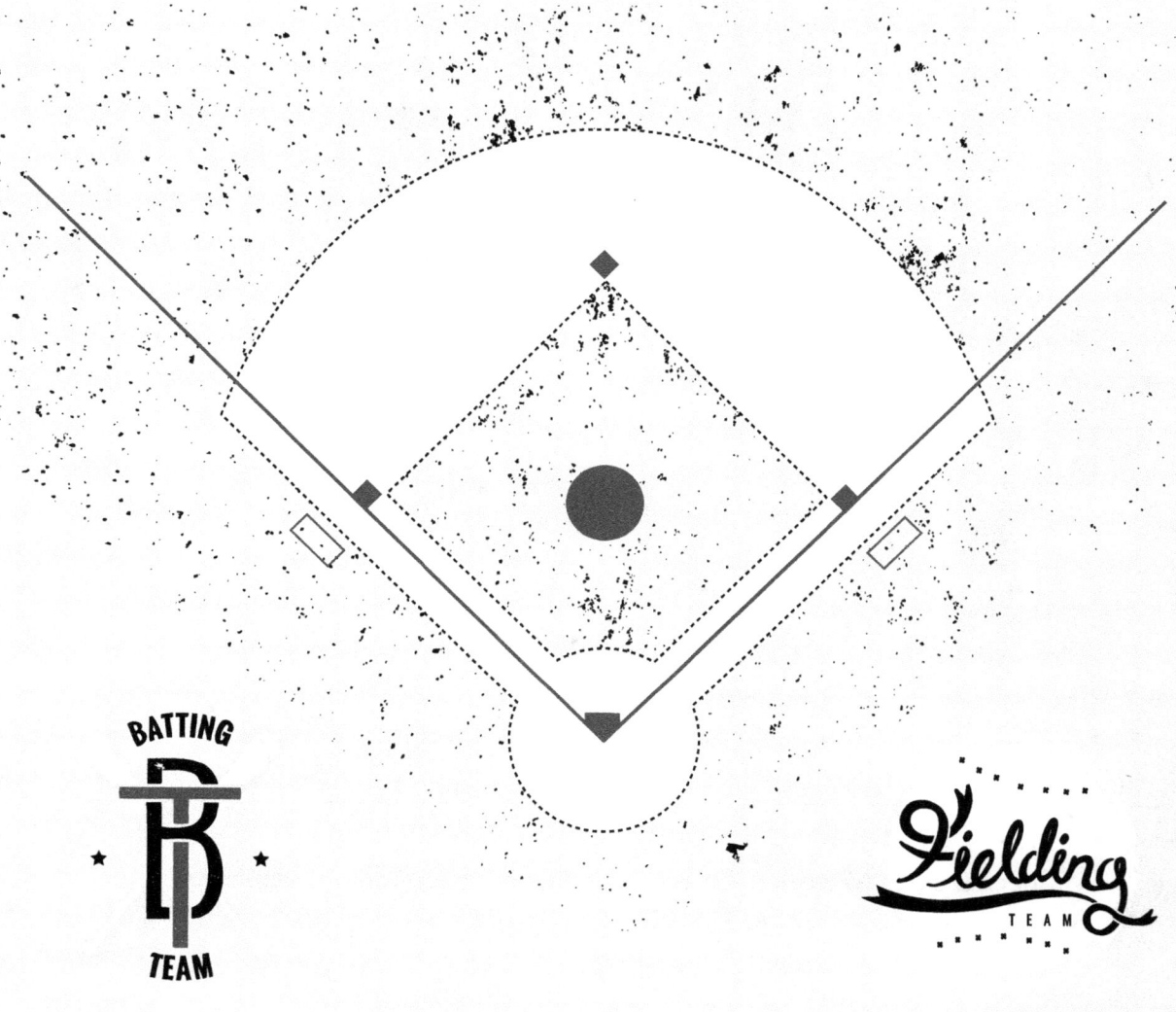

3 PTS

2 PTS

1 PT

3 PTS

2 PTS

1 PT

SCENARIO:

_____

_____

_____

_____

Points to discuss in regards to tactical decisions made by the teams:

_____

_____

_____

_____

_____

Specific skills to work on as identified from observing the scenarios:

_____

_____

_____

_____

_____

_____

	SCORE		
OUTS	FIELDING	INNINGS	RUNNERS
	BATTING		

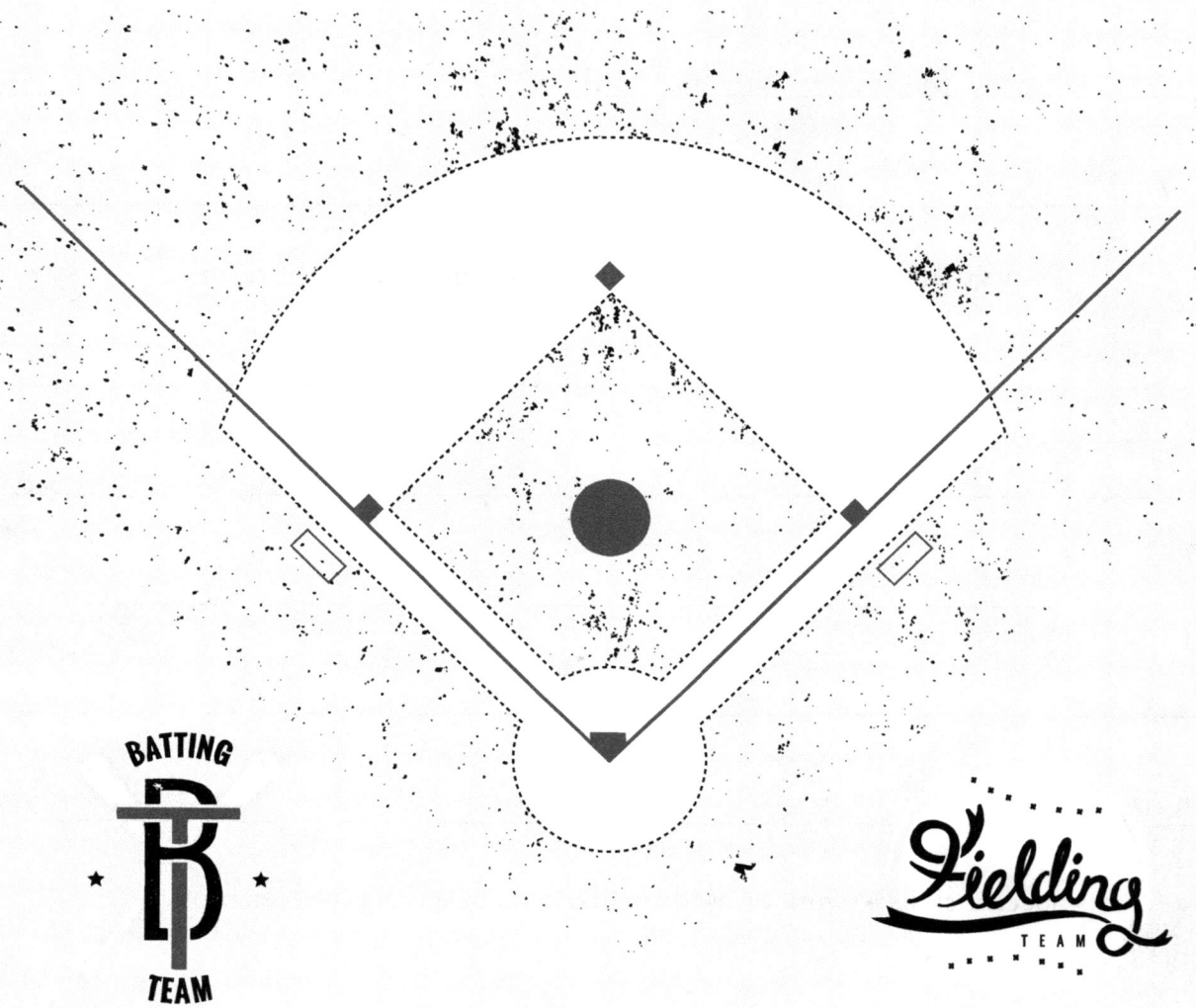

BATTING TEAM

FIELDING TEAM

	3 PTS
	2 PTS
	1 PT

	3 PTS
	2 PTS
	1 PT

SCENARIO:

_____

_____

_____

_____

Points to discuss in regards to tactical decisions made by the teams:

_____

_____

_____

_____

Specific skills to work on as identified from observing the scenarios:

_____

_____

_____

_____

SCORE

OUTS	FIELDING	INNINGS	RUNNERS
	BATTING		

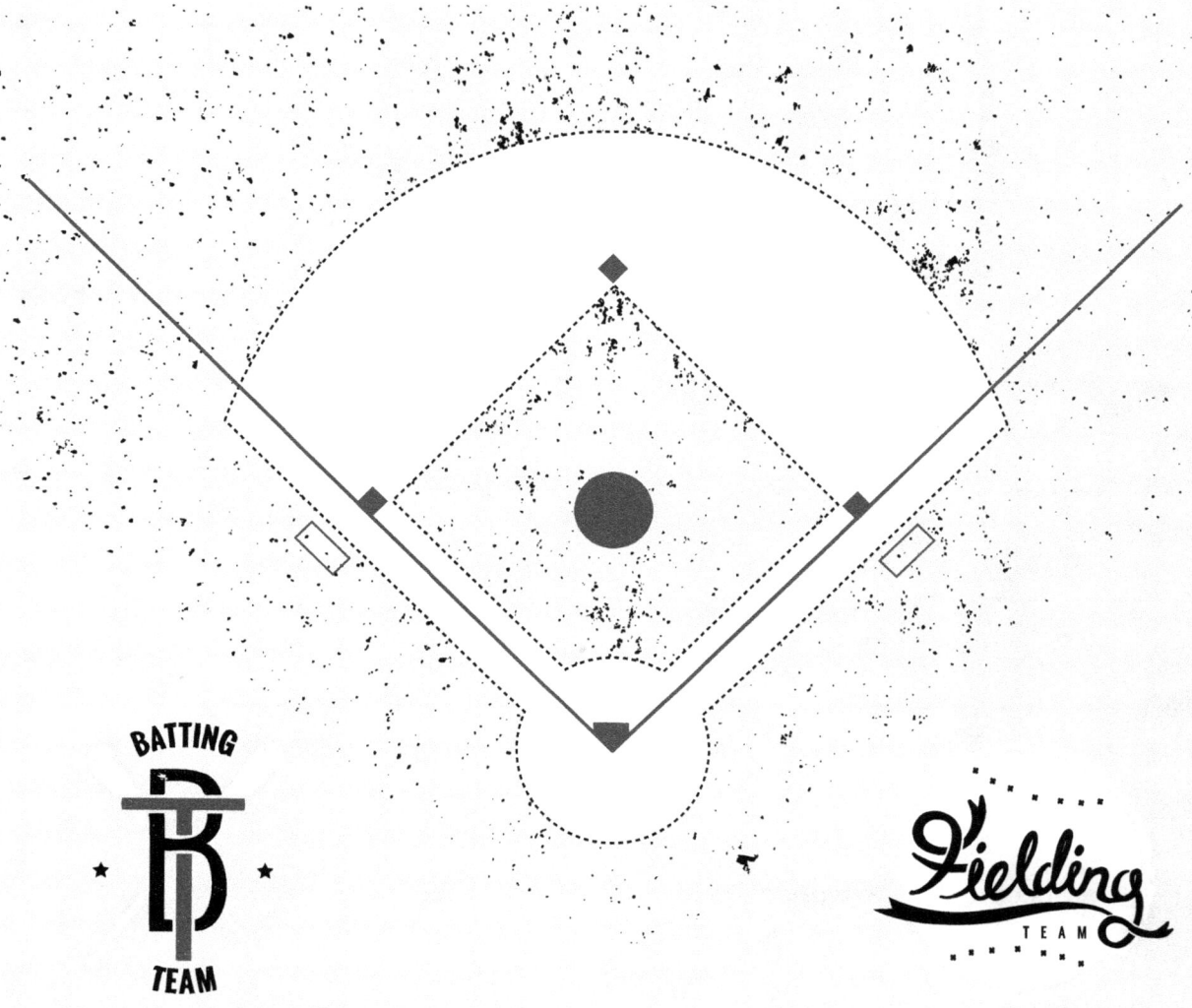

	3 PTS
	2 PTS
	1 PT

	3 PTS
	2 PTS
	1 PT

SCENARIO:

_____
_____
_____
_____

Points to discuss in regards to tactical decisions made by the teams:

_____
_____
_____
_____

Specific skills to work on as identified from observing the scenarios:

_____
_____
_____
_____
_____

SCORE

OUTS	FIELDING	INNINGS	RUNNERS
	BATTING		

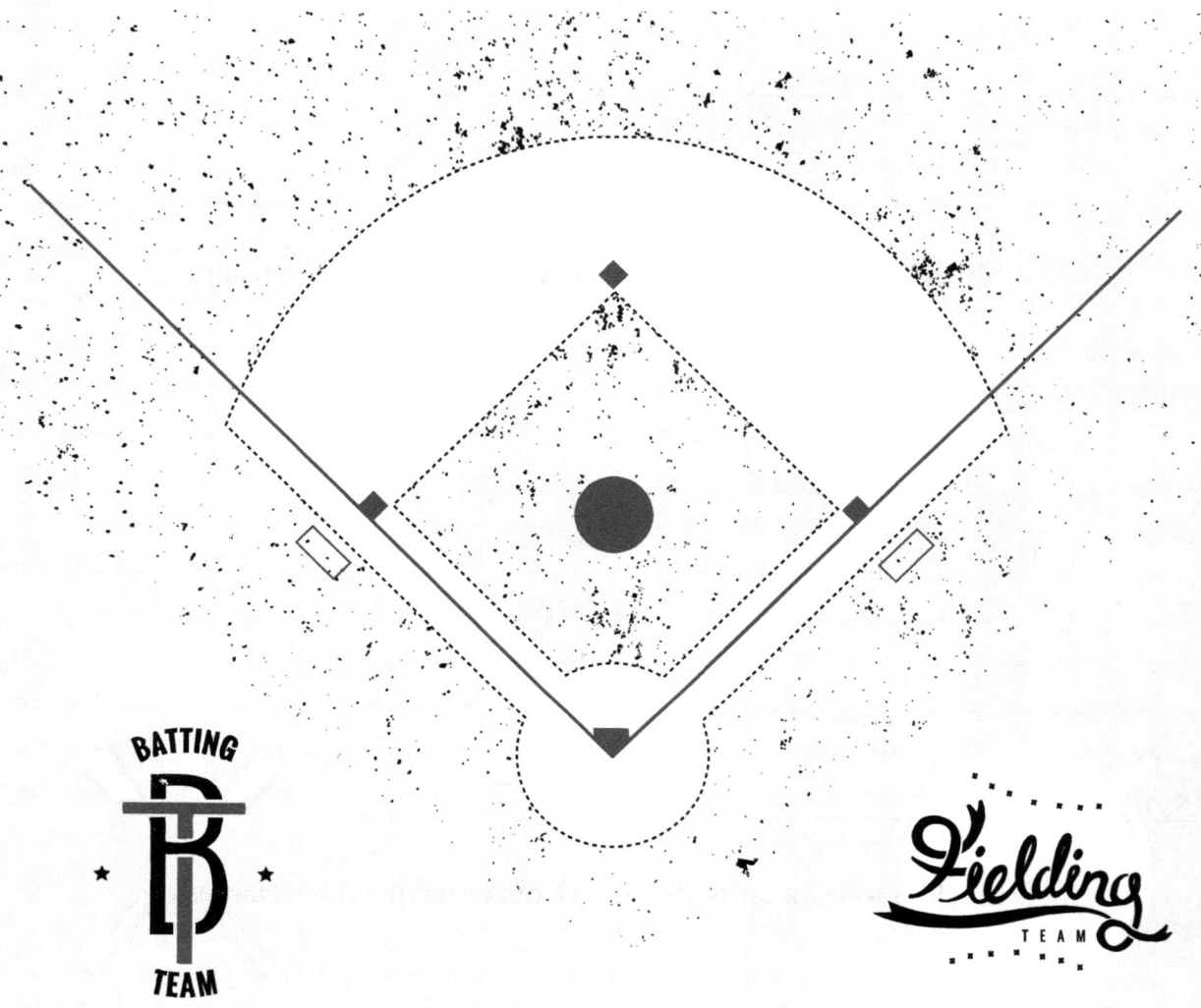

	PTS
	3
	2
	1

	PTS
	3
	2
	1

SCENARIO:

_____

_____

_____

_____

Points to discuss in regards to tactical decisions made by the teams:

_____

_____

_____

_____

Specific skills to work on as identified from observing the scenarios:

_____

_____

_____

_____

SCORE

OUTS	FIELDING	INNINGS	RUNNERS
	BATTING		

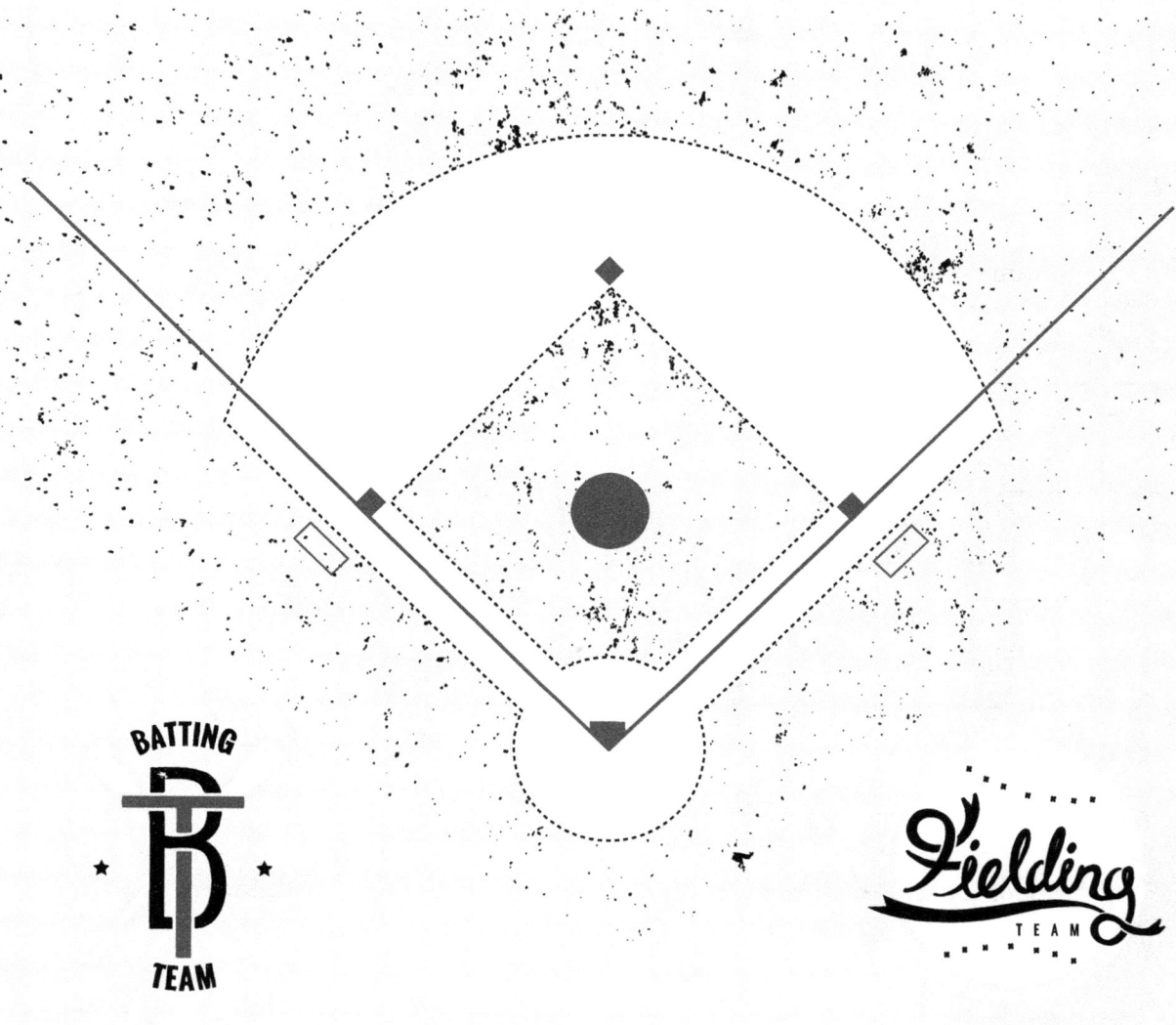

BATTING TEAM

Fielding TEAM

	3 PTS
	2 PTS
	1 PT

	3 PTS
	2 PTS
	1 PT

SCENARIO:

_____
_____
_____
_____

Points to discuss in regards to tactical decisions made by the teams:

_____
_____
_____
_____
_____

Specific skills to work on as identified from observing the scenarios:

_____
_____
_____
_____
_____
_____

SCORE

OUTS	FIELDING	INNINGS	RUNNERS
	BATTING		

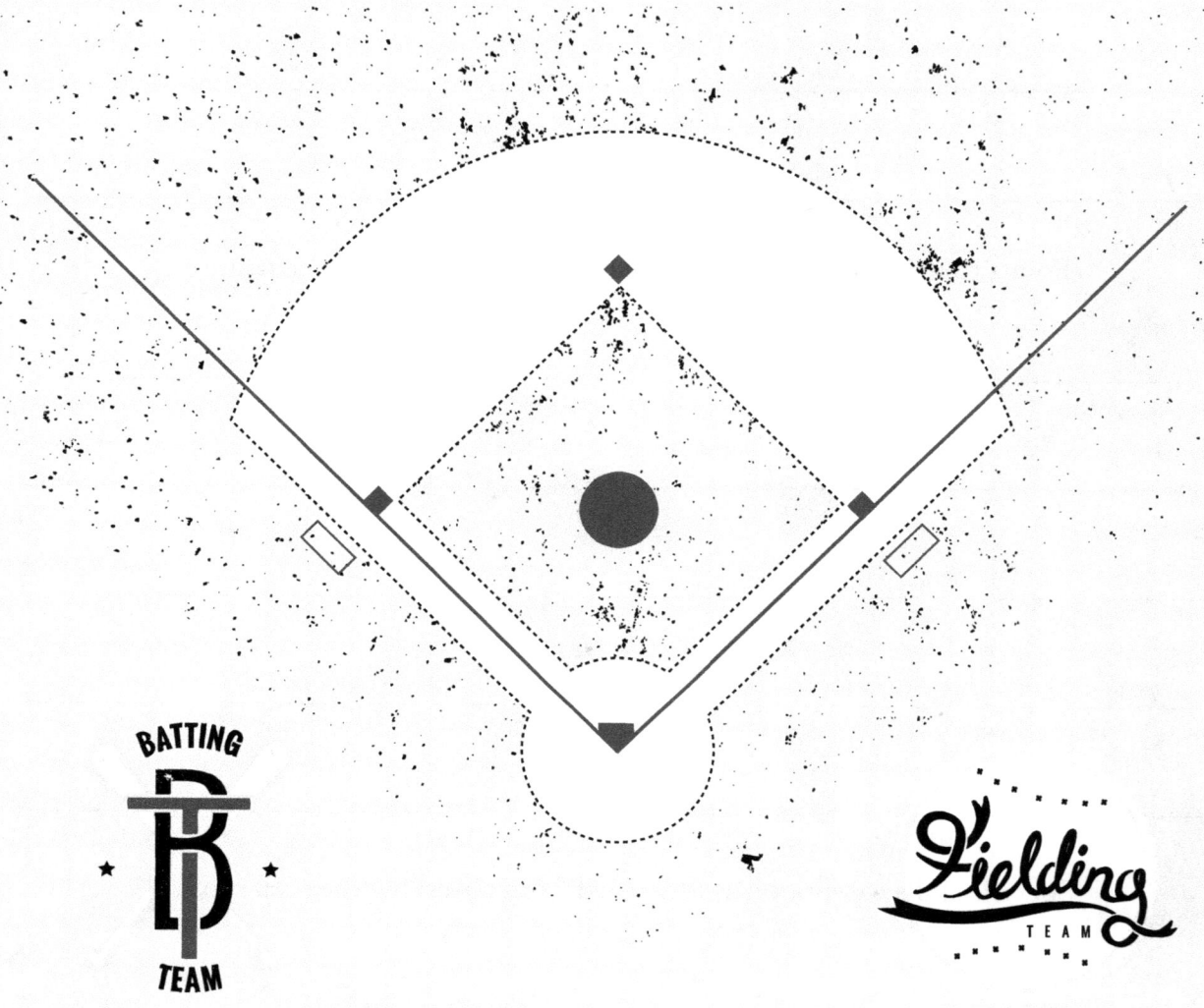

	3 PTS		3 PTS
	2 PTS		2 PTS
	1 PT		1 PT

SCENARIO:

_____
_____
_____
_____
_____

Points to discuss in regards to tactical decisions made by the teams:

_____
_____
_____
_____
_____

Specific skills to work on as identified from observing the scenarios:

_____
_____
_____
_____
_____
_____

AVAILABLE ON AMAZON SOON:

Teaching Games for Understanding
(TGfU) book for coaches and teachers

by Barrie Gordon, PhD.

EXCERPT

2. Change Rules to Encourage understanding

This principle concerns the process whereby secondary rules are introduced to help players develop an understanding of the tactical problems being posed and to reward players who play tactically well. These rule changes are often introduced to increase the probability that the player will discover the correct response. A very successful rule change was instigated by a group of students asked to create games that developed tactical understanding of the benefits of using width in invasion games. They used the context of indoor soccer and introduced two exclusion zones, one on each side of the gym. The zones were about a metre wide and ran the full length of the gym. The rule was that the team with possession had exclusive control of the two zones. This meant that if they could get the ball to a team member in one of the side zones they could not have it taken off them. Teams very quickly started to look for the pass to a free team member in the zone who then either passed it back into play or dribbled it toward the opposition goal until an opening arose to pass to a striker.

Another form of rule changing is based on the idea of removing the constraints brought about by a lack of skill. This principle is important because when players are trying to develop tactical awareness they need to be able to concentrate on understanding the tactical problems, to think through ways of addressing them and to be skilful enough to put the tactics into practice.

An example of this principle was introduced by Rod Thorpe during a visit to New Zealand. Using the context of badminton, he was interested in developing players understanding of moving their opponent around the court to create space in which to win the point. This tactic involved placing the shuttle deep to the back of the court and close to the net, an up and back movement that is a basic tactic of many net games. Implementation of this tactic is however restricted for many as it requires a skilful player to be able to hit a shuttle the full length of the court, especially from deep in their own court.

Thorpe addressed the constraints of this lack of skill by introducing a volleyball into the game to replace the racket and shuttle. Players played one on one on half of the badminton court. The volleyball was served from behind the service line and had to at least reach the opposite service line. The ball was then thrown back and forward until a player scored by getting the ball to hit the floor within the opponents court. A player was allowed only one step after catching the ball and could take up to three seconds before throwing the ball back. This game taught players about moving the opposition around the court, court coverage in defence, the value of clearing deep to gain time, the value of the drop shot and a number of other tactics.

Another example could be a coach working with a hockey or soccer team who is attempting to develop the concept of passing to space. If the players are at a stage where they are not automatically able to trap the ball and pass accurately to a team mate then the players development of tactical understanding will be constrained by this lack of skill. The TGfU approach would look to remove these constraints through rule changes.

For example:

- A game could be played with an implement caught and passed by hand

- A suitably sized ball could be caught and then rolled to a team mate

- If using hockey sticks and balls the players could trap the ball with the foot and either pass with the stick or roll the ball by hand

- Anything appropriate you come up with

It is important in the above examples to focus on what the coach is trying to achieve. At this point all concentration should be on the development of tactical appreciation not the adult rules of a particular game. The games above may be criticised by some because of the obvious breaking of the rules of the adult game. This loses sight of the objective of this approach. Players obviously will be made aware of the adult rules if and when this is needed. Be confident at this point that the game you have designed is a legitimate game in its own right. Don't get the idea that this is not a real game but just something to play until you get to the "real game". Think about backyard cricket. It's a game with its own rules and traditions and a game in its own right, we don't think it is something to play until we get a chance to play 'properly". So to with the games that you develop to play with your classes/teams.

www.ingramcontent.com/pod-product-compliance
Lightning Source LLC
Chambersburg PA
CBHW050503110426
42742CB00018B/3358